When God Says No

Finding Faith in Disappointment

When God Says No

Finding Faith in Disappointment

Bishop Bobby Henderson

Contents

Foreword

In "When God Says No: Finding Faith in Disappointment," Bishop Bobby Henderson offers a compassionate and heartfelt guide to help readers navigate the emotional and spiritual struggles that come with divine denials. As believers, God's "no" or "not yet" can feel like our world has been turned upside down, leaving us feeling confused, dejected, unsure, and unsettled. Simply put, it doesn't feel good. We often wrestle with the pain of wondering why our heartfelt pleas, prayers, and cries seem to go unheard and unanswered. Yet, as Bishop Henderson powerfully illustrates, these moments of divine denial are often profound opportunities for deeper faith and spiritual growth—a chance to trust God's sovereign wisdom, even when we cannot understand His ways, and to trust His heart, even when we cannot see His hand.

Bishop Henderson doesn't shy away from the hurt that accompanies disappointment. Instead, he validates the pain while guiding readers toward a deeper understanding of God's purpose in and for their lives. Much like Job, we may not always receive the answers we desire, but Henderson encourages us to lean into our faith, knowing that God is still present and working all things for our good.

This book is a beacon of hope for those feeling lost or forsaken. It challenges believers to embrace a faith that extends beyond the immediate and to trust a God who operates outside the confines of time and circumstance—one who sees far beyond our limited perspective. In these pages, Bishop Henderson shows us how to find peace in surrendering to God's perfect plan, even when His answers are hard to accept, ultimately leading to a stronger, more resilient faith.

— Bishop J. Drew Sheard

A Testimony of Faith and Resilience

In the stillness of reflection, I find myself overwhelmed by the goodness of God—not because my path has been easy, but because, in every step, He has been there. My story is not one of miraculous recovery or a sudden healing that defies all odds, but rather, it is a testament to unwavering faith in the face of unimaginable trials.

It began in April 2021. I remember that day vividly—April 24th. I had been hopping around on my left foot for some time, enduring the pain and hoping it would pass. But eventually, my wife and I decided that it was time to seek medical help. In the emergency room, the doctor looked at me with a seriousness I hadn't expected. "When did you get this ulcer on the bottom of your foot?" he asked. I was shocked to hear that it was infected—so badly that there was green tissue in it. The doctors warned me that I might face amputation, a possibility that felt like a nightmare unfolding before me.

As a man of faith, I have always believed in the healing power of prayer. I had prayed for countless others over the years and witnessed God perform miraculous healings—restoring the sick, mending broken hearts, and bringing hope to the hopeless. So, I did what I had always done: I prayed. I prayed fervently, asking God to heal my foot as He had healed so many through my ministry. Yet, despite my prayers, the infection worsened. The doctors told me that I had a choice: undergo an amputation or risk losing my life.

On July 21, 2021, my left foot was amputated. I had done everything possible—hyperbaric treatments, vascular surgeries, multiple operations to restore blood flow—but nothing worked. When I woke up from surgery, I felt both relief and a deep, indescribable sorrow. I started the long road to recovery, learning to walk again with a prosthetic, determined to keep serving God and His people.

But then, almost a year later, I looked down at my right foot and saw that my baby toe was infected. I did everything the doctors advised; I managed my diabetes, and I took care of myself. Yet, the infection spread from my baby toe to the rest of my toes. Again, I was faced with the devastating news that another amputation was necessary. On June 9, 2022, at Emory Midtown Hospital, my right foot was removed.

I am a man of faith. I have prayed for hundreds, if not thousands, of people, and I have seen God move in miraculous ways. Yet, my own healing did not come. I struggled to understand why. I wrestled with questions that had no answers, but through it all, I discovered a profound truth: God's goodness is not contingent upon my circumstances. He is good in the healing, and He is good in the suffering.

Hebrews 11:13 reminds us that "These all died in faith, not having received the promises." I have come to understand that while some are healed in this life, others wait for their healing on the other side of eternity. I may not have received the miracle I prayed for, but I have received something even more precious: a deeper understanding of God's unwavering goodness.

There were moments of sorrow, times when the tears flowed freely, and I could not make sense of what was happening. But in those moments, I felt the comfort of God's presence more than ever before. I was blessed to speak with a dear friend and fellow bishop, Bishop Wollard, who had both of his feet amputated over twenty years ago. His encouragement reminded me that God still has a purpose for me, even in this new reality.

Today, I remain in a wheelchair, still believing for the day I will walk again, unassisted. My journey continues with frequent trips to the hospital to drain fluid from my chest, battling heart failure and the aftermath of two heart attacks. The doctors have performed a procedure to clear blockages in my heart, giving me another chance at life. And for that, I give God all the glory.

So, to anyone reading this, I want you to know that no matter what you are facing, no matter how deep your pain or how uncertain your future may seem, God is still good. Even when the healing doesn't come in the way we expect, His presence is the miracle that sustains us. Keep believing, keep trusting, and know that through it all, He is with you.

God bless you,
Bishop Bobby Henderson

Introduction

Life has a way of surprising us, doesn't it? We make plans, set goals, and hold on tightly to faith, hope, and love, believing that God has a grand plan for our lives. As Christians, we trust that our journey is guided by a divine hand, one that leads us toward a future filled with promise and purpose. But then come those unexpected moments—the twists and turns, the valleys and shadows—when our expectations crumble, and we're left grappling with disappointment. It's in these moments that trust in God feels like the ultimate test. How do we navigate these spiritual crossroads? How do we find peace when our prayers go unanswered, our hopes unmet, and our faith feels stretched to its limits?

This book is not an exposition of theological doctrines, nor is it a guide filled with simple answers to life's toughest questions. Rather, it is a heartfelt exploration of what I like to call "divine disappointment"—those moments when our lived reality seems to clash with what we believe God has promised us. It's about finding the courage to trust when the answers aren't clear and the patience to endure when relief seems distant. It's about learning to live with faith in a world that often challenges it.

We all know what it's like to face divine disappointment. It may come as a prolonged illness that defies all prayers for healing, a broken relationship that shatters our dreams of the future, or a door slammed shut when we were sure it was God's will for us to walk through. It's those times when we feel abandoned, wondering if God is really listening—or if He even cares at all. The pain of unanswered prayers can feel like a wound to the soul, shaking the very foundation of our relationship with God.

But what if these moments of disappointment are not signs of God's absence, but invitations to encounter Him in a deeper way? What if the silence we dread is an invitation to lean in closer, to listen more carefully, and to trust more fully? What if our unfulfilled hopes are not evidence of divine neglect but markers along a path that leads to greater understanding and more profound faith?

Throughout this book, we will explore these questions together. We will begin by acknowledging the pain of unanswered prayers and navigating the emotional aftermath of divine disappointment. We will look into the mystery of miracles—why they happen sometimes and not others—and how we can live in the tension of the "not yet." We will confront our doubts and ask tough questions about God's sovereignty, searching for meaning in the midst of our confusion.

We'll also turn to the wisdom found in Scripture, drawing lessons from those who have walked this road before us. The Apostle Paul, who begged for his "thorn in the flesh" to be removed but instead was given grace sufficient for his need. David, a man after God's own heart, who cried out in anguish when his child with Bathsheba was taken despite his desperate prayers. Their stories, like our own, are filled with moments of divine disappointment—but also with the presence and faithfulness of God.

Our journey will also lead us to reconcile faith with reality, recognizing that God's promises may not always align with our immediate desires but are always aligned with His greater purposes. We will learn how to trust that "all things work together for good" (Romans 8:28), even when it doesn't seem so, and to move forward with faith by reframing disappointment as divine direction.

Through each chapter, my hope is that you will find strength, peace, and renewed hope in God's purposes, even when they are hard to understand. You may not have all the answers, and that's okay. Faith isn't about certainty; it's about trust. Trust that God's love is deeper than our doubts, that His wisdom is greater than our confusion, and that His plans are more beautiful than our most cherished dreams.

This book is an invitation to journey together through the highs and lows, the victories and the setbacks, with hearts open to discovering God's presence in all of it. We will learn to embrace the mystery, to find God in both the answered and the unanswered, the miraculous and the mundane. It's about cultivating a faith that endures, a faith that sees beyond the immediate, and a faith that holds firm, no matter how fierce the storms may be.

As we embark on this path together, let us make room for vulnerability, for questions, for honesty, and for the raw, unfiltered conversations that bring healing to our souls. Let us lean into God's promises, even when they seem distant, and find comfort in His unwavering love. Life's uncertainties will surely bring unexpected challenges, but they also offer an unparalleled opportunity to deepen our relationship with the Almighty, especially when He appears silent. Every step, every tear, every unanswered prayer is a part of a divine tapestry being woven just for us—a tapestry of grace, growth, and unexpected beauty.

So, let us walk this road together, not as those who have all the answers, but as those who are willing to trust the One who does. Let us find comfort in His promises, strength in His presence, and hope in His love, even when the way forward is unclear. And let us remember, above all, that we are never alone. God is with us, in the waiting, in the wondering, and in the walking. Always.

1
Facing Divine Disappointments

LIFE AS A believer brings moments of profound peace and joy, anchored in the belief that God is guiding our steps and holding us securely in His hands. Yet, we also encounter seasons that challenge the very core of our faith—those times when our most fervent prayers seem to vanish into the silence, when our cries for help echo back to us unanswered. These moments of divine disappointment are not just difficult; they can feel disorienting, making us question the very foundation of our trust in God.

When we confront these experiences, it often feels like standing in a storm with no clear shelter in sight. Each gust of wind strips away a piece of the confidence we once held. The ground beneath feels less stable, the future more uncertain, and we wonder if the God we believed in is truly listening. It is not a lack of faith that brings these questions; it is the reality of living in a world where pain and suffering are unavoidable. Even the most faithful hearts can find themselves wrestling with doubt in the face of divine silence.

We tend to associate God's love and favor with visible blessings—the healed body, the restored relationship, the open door that aligns with our dreams. But when the healing doesn't come, when the relationship remains fractured, or when every door seems to close, we are left standing at a crossroads of faith. We wonder if God has heard us at all or if His answer is a resounding "no." In these moments, we must confront our assumptions about how God works and what His love looks like.

The Bible is filled with stories that reflect this tension. Moses stood at the edge of the Promised Land, knowing he would never enter because of his disobedience. Hannah wept bitterly for years over her barrenness before she finally saw her prayers answered. David, known as a man after God's own heart, spent years running from his enemies, pleading for deliverance. Even Jesus experienced this kind of divine disappointment in the Garden of Gethsemane when He prayed for the cup of suffering to pass from Him, yet still submitted to the Father's will.

These stories remind us that divine disappointment is not a sign of God's absence or lack of concern. Instead, they show us that every believer, no matter how faithful, must face moments when God's ways are beyond understanding. It is in these moments that we are invited to a deeper trust—a trust that is not dependent on what God does but on who He is.

When prayers seem to go unanswered, it is crucial to allow ourselves to feel the full weight of our emotions. God does not require us to hide our pain or pretend that we are not hurting. He invites us to bring our grief, our anger, our confusion, and our sorrow before Him. He is a God who knows the depths of human emotion and meets us there. We see this truth in the psalms, where David pours out his heart with raw honesty, questioning, pleading, and lamenting before God.

This kind of honest relationship with God is what He desires. He does not ask us to come to Him with polished words or perfect faith. He asks us to come as we are, with all our doubts and fears laid bare. The Bible tells us that He is "near to the brokenhearted and saves those who are crushed in spirit" (Psalm 34:18). He is not distant or indifferent to our suffering; He is intimately present in the midst of it.

Holding onto hope in these moments is perhaps the hardest thing to do. When our prayers seem unanswered, hope can feel fragile, like a thread easily broken by the weight of disappointment. Yet hope is what keeps us moving forward. Hope is what keeps us looking to God, even when everything in us wants to turn away. Hope is what reminds us that God is still at work, even when we cannot see or understand His plan.

We are often tempted to view prayer as a transaction: if we pray the right way, with enough faith, God will respond in the way we desire. But prayer is not about securing specific outcomes; it is about aligning our hearts with God's will. It is about seeking intimacy with Him, knowing that He is good, even when His answers do not match our expectations. Prayer is not a tool to change God's mind; it is a means to change our hearts, to draw us closer to the One who loves us beyond measure.

It is also important to remember that God's silence is not necessarily a denial. Sometimes, what feels like a "no" is simply a "not yet." Other times, the answer comes in a form we did not expect or do not immediately recognize. The story of Lazarus is a powerful example: Jesus delayed coming to heal Lazarus, allowing him to die, only to perform an even greater miracle by raising him from the dead. What seemed like divine inaction was actually an opportunity for God to reveal His glory in an unexpected way.

We must also learn to look for the subtle signs of God's presence, the small miracles that often go unnoticed. A timely word from a friend, a sense of peace that comes in the midst of chaos, or the strength to endure when we feel we have nothing left—these are all signs that God is with us, working behind the scenes in ways we may not immediately perceive. Sometimes, the greatest miracles are not the ones that change our circumstances but the ones that change our hearts.

Navigating these experiences means learning to trust that God's plans are greater than our understanding. Isaiah 55:8-9 reminds us, "For my thoughts are not your thoughts, neither are your ways my ways," declares the Lord. "As the heavens are higher than the earth, so are my ways higher than your ways and my thoughts than your thoughts." Trusting God's higher ways means surrendering our need for immediate answers and resting in the knowledge that He sees the bigger picture.

In this space of divine disappointment, we find ourselves stretched between what we know of God's character and the reality of our circumstances. It is a painful, often lonely place, but it is also a place where our faith can grow deeper and stronger. Here, we learn to cling to God, not because of what He gives, but because of who He is. We learn to trust in His goodness, even when we cannot see His hand.

The Heartbreak of Unanswered Prayers

There is a profound sorrow that grips the soul when prayers seem to go unanswered. It's the kind of sorrow that feels almost physical, an ache deep within the chest that refuses to subside. We have all been there—kneeling in prayer, pouring out our hearts to God, believing that He will respond, only to be met with a silence that seems almost cruel. It's a silence that makes us wonder if our prayers have been lost somewhere between earth and heaven, if they've fallen on deaf ears.

The silence of unanswered prayers can feel like a void, a dark space where hope seems to dwindle with each passing day. It's not just the absence of an answer; it's the sense that God, in whom we have placed our deepest trust, has chosen not to intervene. This is where the heartbreak sets in—the realization that what we have asked for may never come to pass, that the miracle we so desperately hoped for may not arrive.

In these moments, it's easy to feel abandoned. We wonder why God, who is all-powerful and all-loving, would allow us to suffer in this way. Why would He not heal the sickness, restore the relationship, or provide in our time of need? We search for answers, but often, none come. The longer we wait, the deeper the questions dig into our hearts.

The Bible is not silent on the subject of unanswered prayers. Throughout its pages, we find countless examples of men and women who faced similar struggles. David, known for his close relationship with God, frequently cried out in frustration: "How long, O Lord? Will you forget me forever?" (Psalm 13:1). His words capture the essence of what it means to feel forgotten by God, to feel that one's prayers have been ignored.

Even Jesus, in His humanity, experienced the anguish of an unanswered prayer. In the Garden of Gethsemane, He prayed fervently, "My Father, if it is possible, let this cup pass from me" (Matthew 26:39). Yet, He knew that His request would not align with the Father's ultimate plan. Jesus understood the cost of surrendering to God's will, even when it meant facing unimaginable pain and suffering.

These biblical examples remind us that we are not alone in our disappointment. They show us that it is okay to question, to lament, and to express our deepest feelings of hurt and confusion to God. It's not a lack of faith to feel this way; it's a natural human response to suffering. God welcomes our honesty. He invites us to bring our brokenness to Him, trusting that He is big enough to handle our doubts, our anger, and our pain.

But even as we bring our heartbreak to God, we are faced with the challenge of trusting Him in the silence. Trusting God when our prayers go unanswered requires a kind of faith that goes beyond our circumstances. It requires us to believe that God is still good, even when life feels anything but good. It is a faith that chooses to see beyond the immediate, to trust that God is working in ways we cannot yet perceive.

Hope is essential in these times, even when it feels like the smallest flicker in the dark. Hope keeps us connected to the truth that God's love for us is unwavering, that His plans for us are good, even when they don't align with our expectations. Hope anchors us when everything around us feels unstable.

As we navigate the heartbreak of unanswered prayers, we must allow ourselves to grieve the loss of what we hoped for. Grief is not a sign of weak faith; it is a natural response to the pain of unfulfilled desires and unmet expectations. Even Jesus wept at the tomb of Lazarus, knowing full well that He would soon raise His friend from the dead. Our tears are not wasted; they are seen by the God who knows our deepest hurts and holds us close in our suffering. Grieving allows us to face the reality of our loss while keeping our hearts open to the possibility of healing and renewal.

In this space of grief, it is important to remember that God is still at work. He is not limited by time or circumstance, nor is He confined to our understanding of what is best. He sees the entire picture, the beginning from the end, and is weaving together a story that is more beautiful and redemptive than we could ever imagine. His silence does not mean He is absent; it may mean He is preparing something far greater than we could ever ask for or think of.

We see this reality echoed throughout Scripture. When Joseph was betrayed by his brothers, sold into slavery, and unjustly imprisoned, it seemed that God was silent. Yet, in time, it became clear that God had been working all along, positioning Joseph to save not only his family but an entire nation. What looked like divine neglect was actually divine preparation. God's plans were far greater than Joseph's immediate circumstances suggested.

In the same way, we must trust that God's delays are not necessarily denials. Sometimes, what feels like a "no" is really a "not yet," or even a "wait for something better." God is not in a hurry; His timing is perfect. He knows when and how to act in our lives in ways that bring about the greatest good for us and the greatest glory for Him.

Yet, while we wait, we are called to remain faithful. To keep praying, even when it feels like our prayers are bouncing back from the ceiling. To keep believing, even when doubt creeps in like a thief in the night. To keep hoping, even when hope seems like a fragile thing. It is in these moments of waiting that our faith is refined and our character is strengthened. We learn to lean into God's grace, to trust in His love, and to find peace in His promises.

Finding peace in the midst of unanswered prayers requires us to surrender our need for control. It means acknowledging that we do not know what is best, but God does. It means laying down our desires and expectations at His feet, trusting that He will work all things together for our good. It means releasing our grip on the outcomes we want and opening our hands to receive what He has in store for us, even when it looks different from what we imagined.

This kind of surrender is not easy. It goes against our natural inclination to hold tightly to what we think we need or deserve. But it is in this act of surrender that we find freedom. Freedom from the weight of unmet expectations, freedom from the fear of the unknown, and freedom to trust in a God who is always good, always faithful, and always working on our behalf.

We may never fully understand why some prayers go unanswered, why some dreams remain unfulfilled, or why some paths seem closed. But we can trust that God is with us in the waiting, in the wondering, and in the weeping. He is a God who sees us, who knows us, and who loves us more than we could ever comprehend. And He is a God who is writing a story in our lives that is filled with His grace, His mercy, and His love.

When we face divine disappointment, we are given a choice. We can choose to become bitter, allowing our unanswered prayers to harden our hearts and turn us away from God. Or we can choose to become better, allowing these moments to draw us closer to Him, to deepen our trust, and to grow our faith. The choice is ours, but the invitation is clear: to lean into God's love, to rest in His promises, and to trust in His goodness, even when life doesn't make sense.

Navigating the Emotional Aftermath

Navigating the emotional aftermath of such a profound loss as losing both of my legs was a test of faith like I had never known. Before this, I had always prided myself on being independent, capable, and strong. To suddenly find myself in a position where I had to rely on others—sometimes for the simplest of tasks—felt like a stripping away of the life I once knew. The physical adjustments were difficult, but it was the emotional toll that truly weighed me down. I found myself grappling with feelings I had never expected: frustration, vulnerability, and even moments of despair.

I had to depend on people in ways I never had before, and it wasn't easy. The independence I had built my identity on felt shattered. There were days when I questioned not just the circumstances but also my place in God's plan. I would ask, "Why, God? Why this?" It was as if the future I had envisioned had been erased, replaced by an unknown that filled me with both fear and frustration. In many ways, it felt like a loss not just of limbs but of the life I thought I would lead.

Yet, even in the darkest moments, I learned that God was still present. The emotional aftermath of my surgery wasn't something I could push through on my own. I had to lean into the truth of God's promises, even when they didn't seem to align with my feelings. I had to wrestle with the raw reality of what it meant to be vulnerable—not just physically, but emotionally and spiritually. There were moments of anger, where I wasn't just grieving my legs, but grieving the version of myself that I had lost.

In the process, I began to understand something I had often preached but never fully lived: that God's strength is made perfect in weakness. I was learning that my value, my worth, and my purpose weren't tied to my physical abilities but to my identity in Christ. It was a painful lesson, but a necessary one. Through it all, I had to trust that God wasn't wasting this experience—that He was somehow working even this for my good.

As I navigated this emotional terrain, I found myself leaning on the truth of Scriptures like 2 Corinthians 12:9, where Paul writes,

"My grace is sufficient for you, for my strength is made perfect in weakness." It was as if God was reminding me that even though I had lost something significant, His grace was more than enough to carry me through. I didn't have to have all the answers. I just had to keep trusting that nothing in my life—including this deep, personal loss—was wasted in God's hands.

There were days when that trust felt impossible. The emotional weight of needing help for things I used to take for granted felt suffocating. But in those moments, I realized that it was okay to feel overwhelmed. It was okay to admit that I was struggling. I didn't have to pretend that I was fine or that I had everything figured out. I had to give myself permission to grieve—not just the physical loss but the emotional and spiritual impact it had on my sense of self.

That permission to feel became the gateway to healing. I discovered that God is big enough to handle my pain, my doubts, and my fears. In fact, He invites us to bring all of it to Him. The Psalms became my constant companion during this time, especially Psalm 34:18, which says, "The Lord is close to the brokenhearted and saves those who are crushed in spirit." Those words spoke life into me when I felt like I had nothing left to give. They reminded me that even when I felt abandoned, God was still near, still holding me together.

As I walked through this process, I came to understand that healing—both emotional and spiritual—does not happen overnight. It is a journey, one that requires patience, grace, and a willingness to let go of the need for control. It required me to surrender to God's plan, even when I didn't understand it. And as I did, I began to see that while I had lost something significant, I was gaining something far greater: a deeper reliance on God, a stronger faith, and a renewed sense of purpose.

I learned that emotional healing is not linear. There are good days and hard days, moments of peace and moments of struggle. But through it all, God remains faithful. He is the God who promises to "restore the years that the locusts have eaten" (Joel 2:25), and I have seen Him begin to restore not just my physical strength but also my emotional and spiritual resilience.

In the end, I realized that this emotional aftermath was not a place of defeat, but a place of transformation. It was here, in the depths of my pain, that God was doing His deepest work. And while the road ahead may still be uncertain, I know that I do not walk it alone. God is with me, and He is working all things together for good—even the things I never would have chosen for myself.

2
The Mystery of Miracles

MIRACLES—THOSE EXTRAORDINARY MOMENTS when the divine intersects with the ordinary, when heaven touches earth in a way that leaves us breathless with wonder. Throughout history, miracles have been a source of fascination, faith, and, yes, even confusion. The Bible is filled with stories of miraculous events: the parting of the Red Sea, the feeding of the five thousand, the healing of the sick, and the raising of the dead. These moments of divine intervention stir our hearts and strengthen our faith, reminding us that our God is a God of the impossible.

Yet, if we are honest, there is a part of us that wonders: Why do miracles happen for some and not for others? Why does one person receive an answer that defies all logic, while another waits in the silence of heaven? What makes a miracle? Is it the strength of our faith, the fervency of our prayers, or simply the mysterious will of a sovereign God? These questions lead us to a place of deep contemplation, where we must grapple with the mystery of miracles.

A miracle, in its truest sense, is not just an event that defies natural law; it is a revelation of God's character and His desire to make Himself known to His people. It is an act of divine grace that transcends human understanding, a moment when God breaks into our world to remind us that He is with us, that He sees us, and that

He cares. Miracles are not just about the suspension of the natural; they are about the manifestation of the supernatural, the unveiling of God's presence in a tangible way.

Consider the miracles of Jesus. Each one was not only a display of divine power but also a sign that pointed to a deeper truth about who He was and what He came to accomplish. When He turned water into wine at Cana, it was more than a gesture to save a wedding celebration; it was a revelation of His transformative power, a sign that He came to bring joy where there was emptiness, abundance where there was lack. When He fed the five thousand, He was not merely filling empty stomachs; He was declaring Himself the Bread of Life, the One who satisfies our deepest hunger. Each miracle was a window into the heart of God, a glimpse of His love and His desire for His creation.

But what about the times when miracles don't come? What about the times when we pray and pray, yet see no change? This is where the mystery deepens. Miracles, by their very nature, are unpredictable. They cannot be summoned by the sheer force of our will or the strength of our faith. They are, ultimately, acts of God's sovereign will, given according to His purpose and plan. And this is where many of us find ourselves wrestling—caught between the hope of what could be and the reality of what is.

Why, then, do miracles happen sometimes and not others? This is a question that has no simple answer, for it plunges us into the depths of God's wisdom and His mysterious ways. The prophet Isaiah reminds us, "For my thoughts are not your thoughts, neither are your ways my ways," declares the Lord (Isaiah 55:8). There is a divine wisdom at work that we cannot fully comprehend, a wisdom that sees beyond the present moment into the eternal scope of God's plan.

Miracles are not arbitrary acts; they are purposeful manifestations of God's will. When God chooses to intervene in a miraculous way, it is not simply to solve a problem or remove a burden; it is to reveal something greater about Himself, to draw us closer to His heart, and to invite us into a deeper relationship with Him. Sometimes, God performs a miracle to strengthen our faith, to show us that He is still in control when everything else seems out of control. Other times, He withholds a miracle to teach us trust, to refine our character, or to align our hearts more closely with His will.

Living with the "not yet" of miracles is perhaps one of the most challenging aspects of the Christian faith. It is a space of tension where we must hold in balance our belief in God's ability to do the impossible with our trust in His timing and wisdom. It is a place where faith is tested, stretched, and, ultimately, deepened. It is a place where we learn to live with open hands, willing to receive whatever God has for us, whether it looks like what we expected or not.

The Apostle Paul knew this tension well. He wrote of his "thorn in the flesh," a painful affliction that he pleaded with God to remove. Yet, God's answer was not the miraculous healing Paul sought, but a deeper revelation of His grace: "My grace is sufficient for you, for my power is made perfect in weakness" (2 Corinthians 12:9). Here, Paul discovered that the absence of a miracle did not mean the absence of God's power. Instead, it was an invitation to experience God's strength in a new and profound way.

We see a similar tension in the story of Lazarus. When Jesus received word that His friend was ill, He did not rush to heal him. Instead, He waited, allowing Lazarus to die. To those around Him, this seemed like a cruel delay, a failure to act in time. Yet, Jesus was not merely concerned with preventing death; He was planning to reveal a greater miracle—the resurrection of Lazarus. "Did I not tell you that if you believe, you will see the glory of God?" (John 11:40). What seemed like divine inaction was actually a setup for a deeper revelation of God's glory.

Miracles, then, are not simply about what God does, but about who God is. They are invitations to see Him in new ways, to understand His character more deeply, and to trust His heart more fully. Sometimes, the greatest miracle is not the one we see with our eyes but the one that takes place in our hearts. It is the miracle of a heart transformed by grace, a life renewed by hope, a soul anchored in peace even amid unanswered questions.

The mystery of miracles invites us into a faith that is not based on what we receive from God but on who we know Him to be. It is a call to trust that He is good, even when life is hard, to believe that He is faithful, even when the miracle doesn't come. It is an invitation to live in the tension of the "not yet," to keep believing, keep praying, and keep hoping, knowing that God is always at work, often in ways we cannot see or understand.

And so, we are left with this profound truth: that whether we witness a miracle or continue to wait in faith, God is with us. He is working all things together for our good and His glory, even when His ways are beyond our grasp. The mystery of miracles is less about understanding the "why" and more about trusting the "Who." It is a journey of learning to rest in the knowledge that we are loved by a God who sees the end from the beginning, who knows our needs better than we do, and who holds us tenderly in the palm of His hand.

May we live in the wonder of that mystery, embracing the miraculous in both the extraordinary and the everyday, trusting in the One who is always faithful, always present, and always good.

Why Miracles Happen—Sometimes

Miracles often arrive when least expected, catching us off guard with their wonder and power. They can transform a moment, a life, or even a community. Yet, one of the most perplexing aspects of miracles is their apparent selectiveness—the reality that they happen for some and not for others, that one person is healed while another is not, that one storm is calmed while another rages on. This mystery can lead to frustration, confusion, and even doubt, causing us to ask, "Why does God choose to perform miracles for some and not for others?"

To understand why miracles happen sometimes, we must first recognize that every miracle is a revelation of God's heart. It is an expression of His nature and a manifestation of His purposes. When Jesus performed miracles, He did so to reveal more than His power; He did so to reveal His character. He healed the blind to show that He is the Light of the World, who opens eyes to the truth. He calmed the storm to demonstrate that He is the Lord over all creation, who brings peace in the midst of chaos. Each miracle was a glimpse into who He is—a loving, compassionate Savior who cares deeply for His people.

Yet, these miraculous moments were not random acts of kindness; they were intentional displays of divine purpose. When Jesus chose to heal a man on the Sabbath, He did so to challenge the legalism of the religious leaders and to proclaim that God's mercy transcends human rules. When He raised Lazarus from the dead, He delayed His arrival to demonstrate that God's timing is perfect, even when it seems delayed to human eyes. Each miracle had a purpose far beyond the immediate need it addressed; it pointed to a greater reality, a deeper truth about God's kingdom and His plan for humanity.

Miracles happen sometimes because they serve a divine purpose that we may not always understand. They are not merely answers to prayers but are signs that point us toward a greater understanding of God's will. Sometimes, God chooses to perform a miracle to strengthen our faith, to remind us that He is still in control, even when everything around us seems to be falling apart. Other times,

He performs a miracle to reveal His power and to draw others to Himself, using the miraculous as a means to build His kingdom and to bring glory to His name.

However, the absence of a miracle does not mean the absence of God's love or attention. Just as God has reasons for performing miracles, He also has reasons for withholding them. Sometimes, He chooses to work in ways that are less visible but no less powerful. He may be accomplishing something deeper in the unseen realms of our hearts, something that a visible miracle could never achieve. He may be teaching us patience, building our character, or drawing us into a closer, more intimate relationship with Him. His ways are not our ways, and His thoughts are not our thoughts (Isaiah 55:8).

In the story of Job, we see a man who cried out for deliverance, who longed for a miraculous end to his suffering. Yet, God did not respond with an immediate miracle. Instead, He allowed Job's faith to be tested, knowing that through the testing, Job's understanding of God would deepen. Job's story reveals that sometimes, the greatest miracles are not the ones that change our circumstances but the ones that change our hearts. The miracle of a heart that still believes, still hopes, and still loves God in the face of suffering is a profound testimony to the world.

This truth invites us to consider that perhaps the question is not, "Why do miracles happen sometimes?" but rather, "What is God revealing through the miracles He chooses to perform?" And equally, "What is He revealing through the ones He chooses not to?" Every miracle, whether seen or unseen, is a revelation of His presence. Every withheld miracle is an opportunity to encounter Him in a different way—to see Him as the God who sustains, who strengthens, and who is enough, even when the answer is not what we hoped for.

It is easy to believe that a miracle is evidence of God's favor, but the reality is that His favor rests upon us regardless of the miracles we receive. His love is constant, His presence is sure, and His promises are true, whether we witness a miraculous healing or continue to live with the thorn in our side. Our challenge is to recognize His hand at work in all circumstances, to see His grace in every situation, and to trust that He knows what is best for us, even when it differs from our desires.

Miracles remind us of God's sovereignty, of His ability to intervene in our lives in powerful and unexpected ways. But they also remind us of our dependency on Him, our need for His guidance, and our trust in His timing. They call us to a deeper faith, one that is not based on what God does for us but on who He is to us. Miracles are moments of divine clarity in a world often clouded by doubt and confusion, and they invite us to look beyond the immediate and into the eternal.

This is the mystery of miracles: that they do not always come when we expect them, that they do not always look like we imagine, and that they do not always answer our prayers in the way we desire. Yet, they are always part of God's greater plan—a plan that is far more intricate and profound than we could ever comprehend. They are a reminder that we are part of a larger story, a story written by a God who loves us beyond measure and who works all things together for our good and His glory.

In moments when we long for a miracle that does not come, we are invited to trust in the One who holds all miracles in His hands. We are called to believe that He is with us in the waiting, that He is working in the silence, and that He is present in the questions that remain unanswered. Our faith is not in the miracle itself but in the God who can perform it—and who knows, far better than we do, when to act and when to wait.

This understanding leads us to a place of surrender, where we acknowledge that miracles are not ours to command but are gifts given according to the wisdom of a loving Father. We may not always understand His ways, but we can trust His heart. For in the mystery of miracles, we find an invitation to know Him more deeply, to seek Him more earnestly, and to love Him more fully, no matter the outcome.

Living with the "Not Yet"

Living in the "not yet" of God's promises is one of the most profound challenges in the life of faith. It is a place where hope and uncertainty coexist, where faith is tested, and where trust is stretched to its limits. This is the space between prayer and fulfillment, between asking and receiving, between the moment we pour out our hearts to God and the moment we see His hand at work. It is a space that requires us to hold onto God's promises, even when everything around us suggests we should let go.

The "not yet" is where the mystery of miracles becomes most apparent. It is the place where we wait for the breakthrough, the healing, the provision that has not yet come. It is where we learn that faith is not merely believing in what we can see, but trusting in what we cannot. It is where we realize that waiting is not wasted time but holy ground, a place where God does some of His deepest work in our hearts.

Throughout Scripture, we see that God often allows His people to dwell in this space of "not yet." Abraham waited decades for the promise of a son to be fulfilled. Joseph endured years of imprisonment and injustice before he saw his dreams realized. The Israelites wandered in the wilderness for forty years before they entered the Promised Land. Even Jesus, in His humanity, experienced the "not yet" as He waited in Gethsemane, knowing that His prayer for the cup to pass would not be answered in the way He desired.

These stories are not just historical accounts; they are profound lessons for us today. They teach us that the "not yet" is not a punishment, but a preparation. It is a time when God is shaping us, molding us, and preparing us for the fulfillment of His promises. It is a time when our faith is refined, when our trust in God is deepened, and when our character is developed. The "not yet" is where we learn to rely not on our own understanding but on God's wisdom, where we learn to trust not in our timing but in His.

Living with the "not yet" requires us to cultivate a posture of surrender. It means letting go of our need for immediate answers and embracing the mystery of God's plan. It means acknowledging that we do not see the whole picture, but trusting that God does. It means believing that He is good, even when our circumstances are not, and that His love for us is unwavering, even when His timing is unclear.

This surrender is not a passive resignation; it is an active choice to trust God in the midst of uncertainty. It is a daily decision to keep believing, keep praying, and keep hoping, even when the answers are delayed. It is a declaration that we will not let the absence of a miracle shake our confidence in the One who holds all miracles in His hands. It is an affirmation that we believe God is who He says He is, even when His actions—or His inactions—are beyond our understanding.

In the "not yet," we are invited to shift our focus from the outcome we desire to the God we serve. It is easy to become fixated on the miracle we are waiting for, to measure God's goodness by whether or not He grants our request. But the "not yet" is an invitation to fix our eyes on Jesus, the Author and Finisher of our faith (Hebrews 12:2). It is a call to seek His presence more than His provision, to desire His will more than our wants, and to rest in His love, even when His answers are delayed.

There is a profound beauty in this waiting, a sacredness in the surrender. For it is in the "not yet" that we discover who God truly is—a God who is faithful, even when we cannot see the way forward. A God who is present, even when He feels distant. A God who is working all things together for our good, even when the good is hard to see. It is in this space that we learn to trust His heart, even when we do not understand His hand.

Living with the "not yet" also means embracing the mystery of God's timing. We live in a world that values immediacy, where waiting is often seen as a waste of time. But God's timing is perfect, and He is never in a hurry. He knows exactly when to act, and His delays are never without purpose. Sometimes, what seems like a delay is actually a divine setup for something far greater than we could imagine. Sometimes, what feels like a "no" is simply a "not yet" or a "wait, I have something better in mind."

This perspective shifts how we wait. Instead of seeing the "not yet" as a burden, we can see it as an opportunity to deepen our trust in God, to grow in patience, and to develop perseverance. We can choose to wait with hope, knowing that God is at work, even when we cannot see it. We can choose to wait with faith, believing that His promises are true, even when they are yet to be fulfilled. And we can choose to wait with joy, finding peace in His presence, even when the answers are still to come.

The "not yet" is also a place of profound intimacy with God. It is where we learn to lean on Him, to depend on His grace, and to rest in His love. It is where we discover that His presence is more precious than any miracle, that His peace surpasses all understanding, and that His joy is our strength, even in the waiting. It is where we find that He is enough, even when we feel we lack everything else.

As we live with the "not yet," we are reminded that our ultimate hope is not in the miracles we seek but in the God who is with us. Our faith is not based on what He does for us but on who He is to us. It is anchored in His character, rooted in His love, and sustained by His grace. It is a faith that says, "I will trust You, Lord, even when I do not see the way forward. I will believe in Your goodness, even when my circumstances are hard. I will wait for You, knowing that You are faithful, that You are good, and that You are enough."

In the "not yet," we find that our waiting is not in vain. We find that God is always at work, that He is always faithful, and that He is always good. We find that His plans are perfect, His timing is flawless, and His purposes are beyond our comprehension. And we find that, in the end, His love is more than enough to sustain us, to carry us, and to bring us through.

Living with the "not yet" is not easy. It requires faith, patience, and a deep trust in God's character. But it is in this space that we grow, that we learn, and that we draw closer to the One who holds all things in His hands. It is in this space that we discover the true meaning of faith—a faith that is not dependent on what we receive but on who we know God to be.

3
Understanding God's Sovereignty

UNDERSTANDING GOD'S SOVEREIGNTY is one of the most profound and challenging aspects of our faith journey. It involves grappling with the reality that God is in control of all things, that He reigns over every detail of our lives, and that nothing happens outside of His will or His knowledge. This truth is both comforting and bewildering. Comforting because it assures us that our lives are not subject to chance or fate, but are held securely in the hands of a loving Creator. Bewildering because it forces us to confront the difficult question: If God is sovereign, why do we experience pain, suffering, and unanswered prayers?

To understand God's sovereignty is to accept that His ways are higher than ours and that His thoughts are far beyond our comprehension (Isaiah 55:8-9). It is to acknowledge that He is the Creator and Sustainer of the universe, who orchestrates all things according to His purpose and plan. Yet, it is also to recognize that His sovereignty does not mean He is distant or detached from our struggles. He is intimately involved in every detail of our lives, and His love for us is deeper than we could ever imagine.

But how do we reconcile God's sovereignty with the reality of suffering? How do we trust in His control when everything around us feels out of control? These are questions that have plagued believers for centuries, and they are questions that each of us must wrestle with in our own hearts. It is easy to trust in God's sovereignty when life is going well, when our prayers are being answered, and when everything seems to be falling into place. But what about when life takes a turn we didn't expect? What about when our prayers seem to go unheard, when suffering persists, and when we are left wondering why?

In these moments, we are often tempted to ask, "Did I do something wrong?" We wonder if our suffering is a result of our own failures, if God is punishing us for something we have done, or if we are somehow outside of His will. This line of questioning can lead to a spiral of guilt and shame, where we begin to doubt not only ourselves but also God's love and goodness. It is a painful place to be, and it is a place where many of us find ourselves at some point in our spiritual journey.

Yet, to understand God's sovereignty is to recognize that His love for us is not dependent on our performance. He does not love us more when we get it right or less when we get it wrong. His love is constant, unchanging, and unconditional. He is not a harsh taskmaster waiting to punish us for our mistakes; He is a loving Father who desires to guide us, comfort us, and draw us closer to Himself, even in our times of doubt and confusion.

The Bible gives us countless examples of individuals who faced suffering not because of their wrongdoing but because of God's sovereign plan. Job was a righteous man who suffered immense loss, not because he had sinned, but because God allowed it as part of a greater purpose. Joseph was sold into slavery and imprisoned, not because of his own fault, but because God was working behind the scenes to position him to save a nation. The Apostle Paul faced countless hardships, not because he lacked faith, but because God was using his suffering to spread the Gospel and to demonstrate His strength in Paul's weakness.

These stories remind us that suffering is not always a sign of God's displeasure. Sometimes, it is a sign of His trust. It is an opportunity for us to participate in His greater story, to become vessels through which His glory is revealed. Understanding God's sovereignty means accepting that there are aspects of His plan that we may never fully understand this side of heaven. It means trusting that He is good, even when our circumstances are not, and that He is working all things together for our good and His glory, even when it doesn't make sense to us.

Understanding God's sovereignty also requires us to surrender our need for control. It means letting go of our desire to manage every detail of our lives and to trust that God knows what is best for us. It means acknowledging that we do not have all the answers, but that He does. It means believing that His plan is perfect, even when it differs from our own, and that His timing is always right, even when it feels delayed.

This surrender is not a sign of weakness; it is a sign of strength. It is an act of faith that says, "God, I trust You, even when I don't understand. I trust that You are in control, even when everything around me feels out of control. I trust that You love me, even when life is hard. I trust that You are with me, even when I cannot see Your hand at work." It is a declaration that we believe in God's goodness, even when we cannot see it, and that we choose to rest in His sovereignty, even when life feels uncertain.

In the pages that follow, we will explore the tension between God's sovereignty and our human experience. We will look at the question, "Did I do something wrong?" and we will discover what it means to surrender control in faith, trusting that God is with us, for us, and working all things together for our good.

Did I Do Something Wrong?

When we face hardships or unanswered prayers, it is natural to wonder, "Did I do something wrong?" This question arises from our desire to make sense of our suffering, to find a reason for the pain we are experiencing. We want to know why things have gone awry, why our prayers seem to fall on deaf ears, and why God appears distant when we need Him most. In our search for answers, we often turn inward, scrutinizing our actions, our thoughts, and our faith. We wonder if we have failed in some way, if we are being punished, or if we have fallen out of favor with God.

This is a question that many of us have asked at some point in our lives. It is a question that can lead to feelings of guilt, shame, and condemnation. It is a question that can cause us to doubt not only ourselves but also the very nature of God's love and grace. Yet, it is also a question that reveals our misunderstanding of who God is and how He operates in our lives.

To understand this, we must first recognize that God is not a transactional deity. He does not operate on a system of rewards and punishments based on our performance. He is not sitting in heaven with a checklist, deciding whether or not to answer our prayers based on how well we have lived up to His expectations. His love for us is not conditional on our behavior; it is unconditional, unchanging, and eternal. He loves us because He is love, and His love is not something we can earn or lose.

When we face suffering, it is not necessarily a sign that we have done something wrong. The Bible is clear that suffering is a part of the human experience, a result of living in a broken world. Jesus Himself said, "In this world you will have trouble" (John 16:33). He did not promise a life free from pain, but He did promise His presence in the midst of it. He assured us that He has overcome the world and that He is with us, even in our darkest moments.

The question, "Did I do something wrong?" is often rooted in a desire for control. We want to believe that if we can figure out what we did wrong, we can fix it and regain control over our lives. We want to believe that we have the power to change our circumstances if only we can identify the mistake we made. But the truth is, we are not in control. God is. And His ways are higher than our ways, His thoughts higher than our thoughts (Isaiah 55:9).

Job's story is a powerful example of this truth. Job was a righteous man who loved God and lived with integrity. Yet, he experienced unimaginable suffering—losing his children, his wealth, and his health—all without having done anything to deserve it. His friends were quick to assume that he must have sinned, that he must have done something wrong to bring about such calamity. But God made it clear that Job's suffering was not a result of his wrongdoing. Instead, it was part of a greater plan, a divine mystery that Job could not fully understand.

We see a similar lesson in the life of Jesus. He was sinless, perfect in every way, yet He endured suffering beyond what any of us could imagine. He was rejected, beaten, and crucified, not because He did something wrong, but because it was part of God's sovereign plan for the redemption of the world. His suffering was not a punishment but a pathway to greater glory.

These stories remind us that suffering is not always a result of personal failure. Sometimes, it is part of a larger story that God is writing, a story that we cannot see in its entirety. Understanding God's sovereignty means accepting that there are aspects of His plan that we may never fully understand this side of heaven. It means trusting that He is good, even when our circumstances are not, and that He is working all things together for our good and His glory, even when it doesn't make sense to us.

When we find ourselves asking, "Did I do something wrong?" we must remember that God's love for us is not contingent on our actions. He does not love us more when we get it right or less when we get it wrong. His love is constant, unchanging, and unconditional. It is a love that pursues us in our pain, that holds us in our confusion, and that never lets us go.

Instead of focusing on what we may have done wrong, we are

invited to focus on who God is—His character, His goodness, His faithfulness. We are called to trust that He is with us, even in our suffering, and that He is working all things together for our good, even when we cannot see it. We are invited to rest in His grace, knowing that we are loved, accepted, and cherished, not because of what we do, but because of who He is.

Surrendering Control in Faith

Surrendering control is perhaps one of the most challenging aspects of understanding God's sovereignty. It requires us to let go of our need to manage every detail of our lives and to trust that God knows what is best for us, even when we do not. It calls us to release our grip on our plans, our desires, and our expectations, and to place them into the hands of a God whose wisdom far exceeds our own. This act of surrender is not a one-time decision but a daily choice, a continual act of faith that acknowledges that God is in control, not us.

At the core of this surrender is a profound recognition that we are not the authors of our own stories. We may write in hopes and dreams, but ultimately, the narrative belongs to God. He is the one who sets the course, who knows the beginning from the end, and who weaves every thread of our lives into His divine tapestry. When we try to wrestle control from His hands, we are essentially saying that we know better than He does, that our plans are more trustworthy than His. Yet, Scripture reminds us, "Many are the plans in a person's heart, but it is the Lord's purpose that prevails" (Proverbs 19:21).

To surrender control is to accept that our perspective is limited, that we do not see the whole picture, and that we cannot possibly understand all that God is doing. It is to recognize that His plans are far greater, more intricate, and more beautiful than we could ever imagine. It is to trust that He is good, even when we do not understand His ways, and to rest in the assurance that He is for us, even when life feels against us.

But surrendering control is not easy. It is often accompanied by fear and uncertainty. We worry that if we let go, we will lose something precious—that if we trust God's plan, we will be left disappointed or unfulfilled. These fears are natural, but they are also based on a misunderstanding of who God is. He is not a God who delights in our disappointment. He is a loving Father who desires our best, who knows what we need even before we ask, and who works all things together for our good (Romans 8:28).

The act of surrender is a powerful declaration of faith. It is saying,

"God, I trust You more than I trust myself. I trust Your plans more than my desires. I trust Your wisdom more than my understanding. I trust Your heart more than my fears." It is an act of relinquishing our need for control and choosing to rest in God's sovereignty, believing that He knows what He is doing, even when we do not.

Surrendering control does not mean that we become passive or resigned to whatever happens. It does not mean that we stop praying, hoping, or desiring. It means that we bring all of our hopes, prayers, and desires before God and say, "Your will be done." It means that we trust God enough to lay down our plans and to take up His, even when they do not align with our expectations. It is an active trust, a dynamic faith that engages with God's purposes and seeks to align our hearts with His.

Jesus Himself modeled this kind of surrender in the Garden of Gethsemane. As He faced the cross, He prayed with great anguish, "Father, if you are willing, take this cup from me; yet not my will, but yours be done" (Luke 22:42). Jesus did not pretend that He was unafraid or unaffected by the suffering that lay before Him. He was honest about His desire to avoid the pain, but He was also fully surrendered to the Father's will. His prayer was one of both honesty and surrender, of expressing His heart while trusting fully in God's plan.

In surrendering, we are not giving up; we are giving over. We are giving over our fears, our doubts, our desires, and our dreams to a God who loves us and knows what is best for us. We are giving over our need to control every outcome, trusting that God is already in the future, working out every detail for our good. We are giving over our worries about what might happen, choosing instead to rest in the peace that comes from knowing that God is sovereign, that He is in control, and that He will never leave us or forsake us (Deuteronomy 31:6).

Surrendering control is also about finding freedom. Freedom from the pressure to have all the answers, to make all the right decisions, and to carry the weight of the world on our shoulders. It is about releasing ourselves from the burden of trying to manage what we cannot control and allowing God to be God in our lives. It is about trusting that He is enough, that His grace is sufficient, and that His power is made perfect in our weakness (2 Corinthians 12:9).

There is a peace that comes with surrender, a peace that surpasses all understanding (Philippians 4:7). It is the peace of knowing that we are not alone, that we are not left to figure things out on our own, and that we are not responsible for making everything happen. It is the peace of knowing that God is in control, that He is guiding our steps, and that He is working all things together for our good. It is a peace that anchors us in the storm, that steadies us in the chaos, and that keeps us rooted in His love.

Surrendering control in faith also opens the door for God to work in ways that we could never imagine. When we let go of our need to control every detail, we create space for God to move in our lives in ways that are beyond our comprehension. We allow Him to surprise us with His goodness, to overwhelm us with His grace, and to show us that His plans are always better than our own. We open ourselves up to the possibility of miracles, to the reality of His power, and to the beauty of His presence.

In this surrender, we find that God is not only in control, but He is also with us. He is Emmanuel, God with us, walking beside us in every step, holding us in every trial, and comforting us in every loss. He is the God who sees, who knows, and who cares deeply for every aspect of our lives. He is the God who invites us to come to Him with all our burdens, to lay them at His feet, and to find rest in His sovereignty.

Surrendering control in faith is not about giving up hope; it is about finding hope in the One who holds our future. It is about trusting that God's ways are higher, His plans are greater, and His love is deeper than we could ever imagine. It is about resting in the assurance that He is for us, that He is with us, and that He is working all things together for our good and His glory.

When we surrender control, we discover that true peace does not come from having everything figured out, but from knowing the

One who does. We find that true freedom is not found in controlling our circumstances, but in trusting the One who holds all things in His hands. We learn that true faith is not about always understanding what God is doing, but about always trusting that He is good.

As we journey through the uncertainties of life, may we learn to surrender our need for control, to rest in God's sovereignty, and to trust that He is always at work, even when we cannot see it. For in surrender, we find strength. In surrender, we find peace. And in surrender, we find a deeper, more profound relationship with the God who is sovereign over all.

4
Reconciling Faith with Reality

AS BELIEVERS, WE are called to live by faith. We read the promises in Scripture, the assurances of God's goodness, the declarations of His power to heal, restore, and provide. We hear testimonies of miraculous healings and extraordinary deliverances, and we hold on to the belief that God can and will do the same for us. Yet, for many of us, there comes a time when our lived reality does not align with these promises. We pray fervently for healing, but the sickness persists. We ask for deliverance, but the trouble remains. We seek clarity, but the fog does not lift. In these moments, we find ourselves at a crossroads, struggling to reconcile our faith with the reality we face.

This tension between faith and reality can feel like a battle within the soul. On one hand, we know that God is able—that He is all-powerful, that He can do all things. On the other hand, we are confronted with a situation that seems unchangeable, a mountain that refuses to move, a storm that does not subside. It is in this place of tension that our faith is tested and stretched, where our understanding of God's promises is deepened, and where we are invited into a more honest, raw, and authentic relationship with Him.

Reconciling faith with reality does not mean denying the challenges we face or pretending that everything is fine when it is not.

It does not mean ignoring our doubts or suppressing our questions. It means bringing all of these before God—our faith and our fears, our hopes and our hurts, our confidence and our confusion—and trusting that He can handle it all. It means learning to hold two truths at the same time: that God is good, and that life is hard; that He is faithful, even when our circumstances seem to suggest otherwise.

We often think of faith as something that is unshakeable, unwavering, a solid rock upon which we stand. But the reality is that faith is also a journey, a process of growth and discovery. It is not always steady; it can waver, falter, and stumble. It is not a denial of reality, but a decision to trust in the One who holds reality in His hands. It is choosing to believe that God is who He says He is, even when life looks different from what we expected.

This chapter invites us to explore what it means to reconcile our faith with our reality, particularly when it comes to the promises of healing, provision, and deliverance. We will dive into what the Bible really says about healing, examining the tension between God's power to heal and the reality that not everyone is healed in this lifetime. We will also explore the relationship between faith, doubt, and the power of honest prayer, learning how to bring our whole selves before God, trusting that He meets us in our honesty and that He honors our faith, even when it is mixed with doubt.

In this exploration, we are invited to move beyond a surface-level faith that only believes when things are going well, to a deeper, more resilient faith that trusts God even in the darkest valleys. We are invited to move from a transactional view of faith—where we believe that if we do everything right, God will give us what we want—to a relational view of faith, where we trust that God is with us, working all things together for our good, even when life doesn't make sense.

As we wrestle with these questions, we are reminded that faith is not about having all the answers. It is about knowing the One who does. It is not about never doubting, but about choosing to trust, even when doubt is present. It is not about receiving everything we ask for, but about believing that God's plans for us are better than we could imagine, even when we cannot see the way forward.

Let us begin this journey by examining what the Bible really says about healing, and how we can hold onto hope while living in the tension of the "not yet."

What the Bible Really Says About Healing

Healing is one of the most profound promises found in Scripture. From the Old Testament to the New, we see a God who heals, who restores, who makes all things new. We read of the Israelites being healed from deadly serpents in the wilderness, of Naaman's leprosy being cleansed, and of countless miracles performed by Jesus and His disciples. These stories fill us with hope, reminding us that God is a healer, that He has the power to restore broken bodies, wounded hearts, and shattered lives.

Yet, as we look around our world today, we see a reality that is often filled with pain, illness, and suffering. We see people who have prayed for healing but have not been healed. We see faithful believers who live with chronic pain, who endure mental anguish, who face terminal diagnoses. And we are left to wonder: What does the Bible really say about healing? Does God promise to heal every disease, every sickness, every brokenness? And if so, why do some remain unhealed?

The Bible does indeed affirm that God is a healer. In Exodus 15:26, He declares, "I am the Lord who heals you." Psalm 103:2-3 proclaims, "Praise the Lord, my soul, and forget not all His benefits—who forgives all your sins and heals all your diseases." In the New Testament, we see Jesus performing countless healings, demonstrating His compassion and His power over sickness and death. He healed the blind, the lame, the lepers, the demon-possessed. He raised the dead and brought hope to the hopeless. His ministry was marked by miraculous healings, revealing His authority and His deep love for those who suffer.

But we also see in Scripture that not everyone is healed, even among those who are closest to God. Paul, the apostle who performed miracles in Jesus' name, had a "thorn in the flesh" that he asked God to remove, but God chose not to (2 Corinthians 12:7-9). Timothy, Paul's spiritual son, suffered from frequent illnesses, yet there is no record of a miraculous healing (1 Timothy 5:23). Even Jesus, who had the power to heal all, did not heal everyone He encountered. In John 5, we read about the pool of Bethesda, where many invalids lay. Jesus healed one man but left many others unhealed.

These stories challenge the notion that God guarantees physical healing in this life for all who have faith. They remind us that while God can heal and does heal, He also chooses not to heal in some cases, for reasons that are often beyond our understanding. This does not mean that He is any less compassionate, any less powerful, or any less present. It means that His purposes are higher than our desires, and His plans are more comprehensive than our immediate needs.

The reality is that we live in a fallen world, where sickness and death are still present realities. While Jesus has defeated the power of sin and death, we are still awaiting the full manifestation of His kingdom, where there will be no more pain, no more tears, no more suffering (Revelation 21:4). Until that day comes, we live in the tension of the "already but not yet"—where we see glimpses of God's kingdom breaking through, but we also experience the brokenness of this world.

This does not diminish God's power to heal; rather, it points to the greater reality that ultimate healing is found in Him alone. While physical healing is a gift, it is not the greatest gift. The greatest gift is the healing of our souls, the restoration of our relationship with God, the forgiveness of our sins, and the promise of eternal life with Him. This is the healing that is guaranteed to all who believe, the healing that can never be taken away, the healing that transcends every earthly affliction.

In this light, we can pray for healing with boldness, knowing that God is able to do immeasurably more than all we ask or imagine (Ephesians 3:20). But we also pray with humility, surrendering to His will and trusting in His wisdom. We recognize that His ways are higher than our ways and that His thoughts are higher than our thoughts (Isaiah 55:8-9). We trust that He knows what is best for us, even when it differs from what we desire.

When we pray for healing, we are invited to pray with both faith and surrender—faith that God can heal, and surrender to His sovereign will. We are invited to bring our requests before Him with confidence, but also to trust that He will answer in the way that is best, whether that looks like the miracle we hope for or the grace to endure.

This understanding frees us from the burden of trying to manipulate God with our prayers or our faith. It allows us to rest in the assurance that He is good, that He is for us, and that He will never leave us or forsake us. It allows us to find peace in His presence, even when the answer is "no" or "not yet."

So, what does the Bible really say about healing? It tells us that God is a healer, that He loves us deeply, and that He is always working for our good. It reminds us that physical healing is a gift, but it is not the ultimate goal. The ultimate goal is to know Him, to love Him, and to trust Him, in sickness and in health, in life and in death. It calls us to live with both hope and surrender, knowing that whatever happens, we are held in the hands of a loving Father who knows what is best for us.

Faith, Doubt, and the Power of Honest Prayer

Faith and doubt are often seen as opposing forces, but in the reality of life, they often coexist. We are taught that faith is the assurance of things hoped for, yet it's not uncommon to find ourselves wrestling with doubt when the things we hope for seem far off. What do we do when we believe, but also find ourselves asking, "Lord, help my unbelief" (Mark 9:24)?

The journey of faith is never a straightforward path. It's filled with moments of clarity and confusion, peaks of confidence, and valleys of doubt. At times, our faith feels strong, grounded in the certainty of God's promises. Yet, there are seasons when it feels fragile, with doubt creeping in, asking questions that seem to have no immediate answers. It's in these moments that we must learn to embrace both faith and doubt, knowing that God is big enough to handle them both.

Throughout the Bible, we find stories of people who, despite their faith, faced deep moments of doubt. Abraham doubted God's promise of a son and took matters into his own hands. Moses doubted his ability to lead, questioning God's call. Thomas refused to believe in the resurrection until he saw Jesus' wounds. These examples remind us that doubt is not the enemy of faith; often, it is a companion that brings us into a deeper, more authentic relationship with God.

Doubt doesn't disqualify us from God's love or His plans. Instead, it reflects our humanity—our attempt to reconcile an infinite God with our limited understanding. It's in these spaces of uncertainty that we are invited to bring our honest questions to God, trusting that He meets us with grace, not disappointment.

One of the most powerful tools in navigating the tension between faith and doubt is prayer—honest, raw, prevailing prayer. Over the years, I have had the privilege of leading countless prayer meetings and shut-ins, witnessing firsthand the transformative power of honest, relentless prayer. In these moments, I've seen doubt laid bare, faith reignited, and lives changed. It's not always about receiving immediate answers, but about encountering the presence of God in the midst of our questions.

Prayer isn't about presenting a perfect version of ourselves to God; it's about bringing our whole selves, with all our doubts and fears, and laying them at His feet. It's about trusting that He hears us, understands us, and invites us into a deeper relationship with Him. We see this in the psalms of David, where he would cry out, "How long, O Lord?" or in Jesus' own words on the cross, "My God, why have You forsaken me?" These raw prayers reflect a faith that dares to be honest with God, trusting that He is near, even in the silence.

In the Garden of Gethsemane, Jesus modeled this type of prayer. He was honest about His fears, yet surrendered to the Father's will. This is the power of honest prayer—it allows us to hold both our desires and our surrender together. It's in these moments of vulnerability that God meets us with His strength, and it's in our weakness that His power is made perfect.

Throughout my years in ministry, I've seen how prayer can move mountains, not just in the physical sense but within the hearts of those who pray. It bridges the gap between faith and doubt, allowing God to speak into our uncertainties and reaffirm His presence in our lives. Even when we don't get the answers we seek, we always get the comfort of His presence, which is often the most profound answer of all.

Faith and doubt are not mutually exclusive. In fact, it is in the presence of doubt that faith often grows. When we bring our honest prayers before God, we invite Him to meet us in our weakness, to reassure us of His love, and to remind us that He is always working, even when we cannot see it.

Let us come boldly before God, with all our doubts, and trust that His presence will sustain us through every question and every season.

5
Lessons from Paul's Thorn

PAUL, A MAN whose faith and perseverance shaped the early church, knew firsthand the reality of suffering. Despite his deep relationship with Christ and his tireless commitment to spreading the gospel, he faced an affliction that persisted—a "thorn in the flesh." This thorn, whatever its nature, was a source of pain and weakness for Paul, causing him to plead with God three times for its removal. Yet, rather than receiving the healing he desired, Paul was given an unexpected answer: "My grace is sufficient for you, for my power is made perfect in weakness" (2 Corinthians 12:9).

The significance of Paul's thorn extends far beyond the immediate context of his life. It challenges the assumption that suffering is always a sign of God's disfavor or a consequence of wrongdoing. Paul's experience reveals that suffering can coexist with deep faith and that God's purposes are often greater than our understanding. His thorn was not a punishment but a profound opportunity to learn reliance on God's grace rather than his strength. In this affliction, Paul discovered that true power is found not in self-sufficiency but in complete dependence on God.

The thorn in Paul's flesh remains a mystery, not because its details are unclear, but because its purpose goes beyond a specific ailment. It represents any struggle, any lingering pain, any situation that seems unresolved despite our fervent prayers. It stands as a universal symbol for the suffering that touches every life, and it calls us to confront our own experiences of pain with an openness to God's deeper purposes. It is in this space of wrestling that we begin to understand that our weaknesses are not obstacles but platforms for God's strength.

Paul's struggle shows that God sometimes chooses not to remove our suffering because He has a higher plan. Paul was given a divine response that redirected his focus from seeking relief to embracing grace: "My grace is sufficient for you, for my power is made perfect in weakness." Through this answer, Paul learned that God's grace was enough to sustain him, that God's presence was greater than his pain, and that God's purpose was being fulfilled even in his weakness. This response invites us to stop trying to escape our thorns and instead to see them as opportunities to experience God's sustaining grace.

The lesson of Paul's thorn is not about passive resignation to suffering but about active trust in God's wisdom and timing. Even in the midst of our most difficult struggles, we are reminded that God is intimately involved in our lives, using every challenge to shape us, refine us, and draw us closer to Him. The thorn was not a barrier to Paul's ministry; it was a catalyst for deeper dependence on Christ. It was a means by which Paul could more fully embody the message of the gospel—a message of strength through weakness, victory through surrender, and life through death.

This understanding of suffering is deeply countercultural. In a world that glorifies strength, independence, and self-reliance, Paul's embrace of his thorn seems almost radical. Yet, it is precisely in his weakness that Paul found the fullness of God's strength. He learned to boast in his weaknesses, to delight in his hardships, and to rejoice in his difficulties, because he knew that in those moments, God's power was at its most visible. "For when I am weak, then I am strong" (2 Corinthians 12:10).

The story of Paul's thorn teaches us that God's grace is always sufficient, no matter what we face. It calls us to trust that God knows what He is doing, even when we do not understand. It challenges us to see our suffering not as a sign of failure but as a place where God's strength can shine most brightly. And it invites us to come to God with our weaknesses, to lay down our pride, and to receive His grace anew each day.

This lesson is not an easy one to learn. It goes against our natural inclination to avoid pain, to seek comfort, and to rely on our strength. But as we open ourselves up to the possibility that God's grace is sufficient, we begin to experience the freedom that comes from knowing that we do not have to be strong on our own. We find that His grace truly is enough, that His power is made perfect in our weakness, and that in every thorn, there is an invitation to trust Him more deeply.

Understanding Paul's Struggle

The Apostle Paul was no stranger to hardship. Throughout his ministry, he faced intense persecution, imprisonment, beatings, and numerous other trials. Yet, despite all of this, Paul remained steadfast in his faith and unwavering in his commitment to proclaim the gospel. He endured suffering with a resilience that inspires believers to this day. But there was one particular affliction that seemed to challenge him more than any other—the infamous "thorn in the flesh."

In 2 Corinthians 12:7-10, Paul describes his struggle: "Therefore, in order to keep me from becoming conceited, I was given a thorn in my flesh, a messenger of Satan, to torment me. Three times I pleaded with the Lord to take it away from me." Paul's language here is raw and personal. He speaks of torment, of pleading, of a persistent affliction that he desperately wanted to be removed. This was not a minor inconvenience; it was a significant, ongoing source of pain.

But what exactly was this thorn? The Bible does not specify, and perhaps that is intentional. By leaving it ambiguous, Paul's thorn becomes a universal symbol of suffering. It represents any affliction—physical, emotional, spiritual, or relational—that we carry and that seems to have no immediate resolution. It is the unanswered prayer, the lingering pain, the chronic illness, the unhealed wound. It is whatever causes us to cry out to God, pleading for relief.

Paul's experience reveals that even the most faithful followers of Christ are not immune to suffering. His thorn was not a punishment for wrongdoing; it was a means of preserving his humility and dependence on God. "To keep me from becoming conceited," Paul writes. In other words, his suffering had a purpose beyond what he could see. It was not arbitrary; it was not meaningless. It was a tool in the hands of a sovereign God, used to shape Paul into the man he was called to be.

This is a difficult truth for many of us to accept. We want to believe that if we are faithful, if we pray earnestly, if we live righteously, God will shield us from pain. But Paul's experience shatters this notion. It shows us that suffering is not always a sign of divine displeasure. Sometimes, it is a sign of divine purpose. Sometimes, God allows thorns in our lives not to harm us, but to help us—to keep us humble, to keep us dependent, to keep us close to Him.

Paul's struggle also teaches us about the nature of prayer and how to approach God in our pain. Notice that Paul did not shy away from bringing his request before God. "Three times I pleaded with the Lord to take it away from me." He was persistent in his prayer, honest in his plea. He did not pretend that he was okay or that he could handle it on his own. He brought his pain to God, trusting that God cared and that God could intervene.

But God's response to Paul was not what he expected. Instead of removing the thorn, God offered something different: "My grace is sufficient for you, for my power is made perfect in weakness" (2 Corinthians 12:9). This was not the answer Paul was looking for, but it was the answer he needed. It was a reminder that God's ways are not our ways, that His thoughts are not our thoughts (Isaiah 55:8-9). It was an invitation to see his suffering from a different perspective—not as a curse, but as a place where God's power could be displayed most beautifully.

In this response, we learn that God does not always answer our prayers in the way we desire, but He always answers in the way that is best. He does not always remove the thorn, but He promises to be with us in it. He does not always take away the pain, but He offers His presence, His peace, and His strength to carry us through.

Paul's experience invites us to bring our own thorns before God—to be honest about our pain, to plead for relief, and to trust in His response. It invites us to see our suffering not as a sign of failure, but as a place where God's grace can be revealed. It invites us to embrace our weaknesses, knowing that it is in our weakness that His strength is made perfect.

This shift in perspective does not make the suffering easier, but it does give it meaning. It allows us to see our pain through the lens of God's purpose, to trust that He is working all things together for our good, even when it hurts. It reminds us that our thorns are not obstacles to be removed but opportunities to encounter His grace in deeper, more profound ways.

The Power of God's Grace in Weakness

The idea that God's power is made perfect in weakness is a truth that runs counter to much of our natural inclination. We live in a world that values strength, self-reliance, and independence. We are taught to hide our weaknesses, to overcome them, to prove that we are capable and competent. But God's kingdom operates on a different principle. In God's economy, it is not our strength that qualifies us for His work; it is our willingness to acknowledge our weakness and our need for His grace.

When God tells Paul, "My grace is sufficient for you, for my power is made perfect in weakness," He is revealing a profound truth about the nature of His grace. Grace is not just God's unmerited favor; it is His active power at work in our lives, enabling us to do what we could never do on our own. It is His strength meeting us in our frailty, His sufficiency filling our inadequacy, His presence sustaining us in our pain.

Paul came to understand that his thorn, far from being a hindrance, was actually a channel through which God's grace flowed most freely. It was in his weakness that he experienced God's strength most fully. It was in his dependence on God that he found true freedom. "Therefore," Paul writes, "I will boast all the more gladly about my weaknesses, so that Christ's power may rest on me. That is why, for Christ's sake, I delight in weaknesses, in insults, in hardships, in persecutions, in difficulties. For when I am weak, then I am strong" (2 Corinthians 12:9-10).

This is the paradox of God's grace: that it shines brightest in our darkest moments, that it is most powerful when we feel most powerless. It is not in our self-sufficiency but in our dependence on Him that we find true strength. It is not in our ability to control our circumstances but in our surrender to His sovereignty that we find peace.

The power of God's grace in weakness is a lesson that challenges us to rethink our understanding of strength. It calls us to let go of our desire to be self-reliant and to embrace our need for God. It invites us to see our weaknesses not as liabilities, but as opportunities for God's power to be displayed in our lives. It reminds us that we do not have to be strong on our own; we only need to rely on the One who is strong for us.

In our culture, weakness is often seen as a flaw, something to be hidden or fixed. But in God's kingdom, weakness is a place of encounter, a place where His grace meets us most intimately. It is in our weakness that we are reminded of our need for Him, of our dependence on His strength, of our reliance on His provision. It is in our weakness that we discover the depth of His love, the reach of His mercy, and the sufficiency of His grace.

The power of God's grace in weakness is also a call to authenticity. It is an invitation to bring our true selves before God, to be honest about our struggles, our doubts, our fears, and our failures. It is a reminder that we do not have to pretend to be perfect or to have it all together. God does not ask for our perfection; He asks for our honesty. He does not demand our strength; He offers us His. He does not require us to hide our weaknesses; He invites us to bring them into the light, where His grace can transform them into testimonies of His power.

When we embrace our weaknesses, we make room for God's strength. When we acknowledge our need, we open ourselves up to His provision. When we surrender our desire for control, we find freedom in His sovereignty. This is the power of God's grace in weakness: that it transforms our pain into purpose, our struggles into testimonies, and our weaknesses into displays of His strength.

Paul's story reminds us that our thorns, our struggles, and our weaknesses are not signs of failure; they are opportunities for God's grace to shine in our lives. They are places where we encounter His love in deeper ways, where we experience His presence more fully, and where we discover that His grace truly is sufficient for us.

As we navigate our own thorns, may we find the courage to bring them before God, to trust in His grace, and to rely on His strength. May we learn to boast in our weaknesses, knowing that it is in our weakness that His power is made perfect. And may we discover, like Paul, that when we are weak, then we are strong—not because of who we are, but because of who He is.

6
Do All Things Really Work Together?

THE PROMISE FOUND in Romans 8:28, *"And we know that all things work together for good to those who love God, to those who are the called according to His purpose"* (NKJV), is both comforting and perplexing. This assurance, that God is weaving every part of our lives into a greater plan, challenges us to trust that He is at work even when circumstances seem bleak or confusing. It calls us to look beyond the immediate and into the eternal, believing that every joy, every sorrow, every victory, and every defeat are part of a story God is writing for our good and His glory. It asks us to hold onto faith, trusting in His greater vision.

Believing that all things work together for good does not mean denying the reality of pain or pretending that everything is easy. It means recognizing that God's perspective is far wider and deeper than our own. It means trusting that He sees the end from the beginning, working in every detail of our lives, even when we cannot see it. This trust invites us to move from fear and uncertainty to faith and confidence, knowing that nothing is wasted in God's hands. Every tear, every prayer, and every unanswered question is part of His purposeful plan, a plan that far exceeds our understanding.

This confidence is not a blind optimism that ignores suffering but a deep assurance that God is present in every circumstance, working behind the scenes to bring about His perfect will. The promise of Romans 8:28 does not suggest a life free of struggle but assures us that, even in our darkest moments, God is working for our good. In every moment, God invites us to trust Him more, to lean into His promises, and to believe that He is actively weaving all things together for a purpose that is ultimately good, even when the path ahead is unclear.

Our human nature tends to question how certain challenges could possibly work together for good. How can illness, loss, or disappointment fit into God's grand design? Yet, Romans 8:28 reminds us that God's definition of "good" isn't always what we imagine. It's not simply about comfort or ease, but about growth, transformation, and bringing us closer to Him. Often, the good God is working in us comes through refining processes—through the fire of trials that strengthen our faith and shape our character. It's in these seasons that God stretches us, preparing us for something far greater than we could imagine on our own.

God's promise that all things work together for good assures us that no part of our lives is wasted. Every joy, every heartache, every success, and every setback are woven into His perfect plan. His sovereignty is at work in ways we cannot always see. This invites us to release our need for control and surrender to His divine orchestration. Even when life feels chaotic, we can trust that God is not only aware but actively involved in every detail, using it for a greater purpose. This faith in His plan requires us to look beyond our immediate circumstances and trust in His eternal perspective.

Trusting in this promise doesn't mean we deny our struggles or pain. Instead, it allows us to face them with confidence that God is still in control. Romans 8:28 calls us to shift our focus from what is happening around us to who God is. It teaches us to trust not in the outcome of our situation but in the unchanging character of God. His goodness is not dependent on our circumstances. It remains constant, no matter what we face. He is always for us, working behind the scenes, and turning every difficulty into an opportunity for His glory.

As we grow in our understanding of Romans 8:28, our perspective shifts. We begin to see our lives through the lens of faith, recognizing that even the trials we face are part of God's refining work. The challenges we encounter are not without purpose; they are opportunities for God to display His faithfulness. In moments of waiting, in the times when prayers seem unanswered, God is doing a deeper work in us. He is shaping us, strengthening us, and preparing us for the good He has planned. These are the moments when our faith grows, as we learn to trust God not only for what He does but for who He is.

Ultimately, Romans 8:28 points us to the heart of God—a God who is good, who loves us deeply, and who is always working on our behalf. He does not promise a life free from hardship, but He does promise that He is with us through it all, turning every trial into a testimony of His grace. This truth brings peace in uncertainty, hope in despair, and a confidence that no matter what we face, God's hand is guiding us toward His perfect will. We can rest in this promise, knowing that in all things, God is working for the good of those who love Him, according to His purpose.

Trusting That Nothing is Wasted

Trusting that nothing is wasted requires a deep and abiding faith in the sovereignty of God. It's the belief that no part of our lives, no matter how painful or confusing, is without purpose in His grand design. This perspective challenges us to look beyond the temporary struggles and hardships we face, focusing instead on the eternal picture God is painting with our lives. It allows us to embrace the idea that everything we go through—both the good and the bad—is being used by God to shape, refine, and mold us into who He has called us to be.

Take the story of Joseph, for instance. On the surface, Joseph's life seemed to spiral out of control. His brothers, driven by jealousy, sold him into slavery. He was later falsely accused of a crime he didn't commit and thrown into prison. From a human standpoint, it seemed like Joseph's life was full of unjust suffering. But God was at work the entire time, orchestrating events for a purpose far greater than Joseph could have ever imagined. Joseph's rise to power in Egypt wasn't just for his benefit; it was part of God's plan to save his family and countless others from famine. What seemed like a series of tragic, wasted years was actually a key part of God's divine strategy.

Joseph's eventual realization of this truth is captured in his words to his brothers: *"You meant evil against me, but God meant it for good"* (Genesis 50:20, NKJV). This revelation is a powerful reminder that God can take what was meant for harm and use it for good. It demonstrates that nothing in our lives is outside of God's reach. He can redeem even the most painful experiences, turning them into something that fulfills His will and glorifies His name.

But trusting that nothing is wasted is not always easy. It often requires us to look past the immediate pain and confusion of our circumstances. When life takes unexpected turns, when we experience loss, disappointment, or injustice, it can be difficult to see how God is working through it all. Our natural inclination is to focus on the problem in front of us, to ask *"Why is this happening?"* or *"How could any good come from this?"* Yet, it is precisely in these moments of questioning that God invites us to trust Him more fully, to believe that He is working all things together for our good.

This trust calls for a transformation in the way we view our circumstances. It challenges us to shift from seeing our struggles as pointless setbacks to recognizing them as stepping stones in our spiritual growth. Every hardship, every trial, every unanswered prayer is an opportunity for God to work in us, to refine our faith, and to deepen our reliance on Him. When we believe that nothing is wasted, we can find peace in the midst of chaos, knowing that God is in control, weaving every moment into His perfect plan.

Another key to trusting that nothing is wasted is the realization that God's purpose for our lives is often much bigger than we can comprehend. Our limited perspective only allows us to see a small part of the picture, but God sees the whole canvas. He knows how every detail fits together, and He is using even the seemingly insignificant or painful parts of our lives to fulfill His ultimate purpose. This understanding can free us from the need to make sense of everything. We can rest in the assurance that God knows what He's doing, even when we don't.

When we embrace this truth, it transforms the way we experience life's ups and downs. We begin to see God's hand at work in both the mundane and the extraordinary. We start to understand that even in seasons of waiting or difficulty, God is using every moment to shape us into the people He has called us to be. Nothing is wasted—not the moments of joy, nor the moments of pain. Everything is part of God's process of making us more like Him.

This kind of trust also brings freedom. It frees us from the burden of trying to control every aspect of our lives, from the pressure to understand why things happen the way they do. Instead, we can surrender to God's plan, confident that He is working everything for good, even when we can't see the full picture. This freedom allows us to walk by faith, trusting that God is guiding our steps, even when the path seems unclear.

Moreover, trusting that nothing is wasted helps us cultivate a heart of gratitude. When we believe that God is using every experience for our good, we can thank Him in all circumstances—not just in the good times, but also in the challenging ones. We can give thanks, not necessarily for the trial itself, but for the work God is doing in us through it. This gratitude shifts our focus from what we've lost to what God is accomplishing, allowing us to see His grace in every situation.

Ultimately, trusting that nothing is wasted deepens our relationship with God. It draws us closer to Him, as we learn to rely more fully on His wisdom and goodness. It builds our faith, as we see Him work through the difficulties of life in ways we never expected. And it brings us hope, knowing that even in our hardest moments, God is at work, shaping our lives for His glory and our good. Nothing is wasted in the hands of a loving, sovereign God.

Seeing God's Hand in Every Season

Life is marked by seasons, each one different from the last. There are seasons of joy, when everything seems to be going right, and seasons of sorrow, when nothing seems to make sense. There are seasons of growth, when we feel God's presence so strongly, and seasons of waiting, when He seems silent. Yet, through it all, God is at work, guiding us, shaping us, and revealing Himself to us in new and unexpected ways.

Seeing God's hand in every season requires a posture of openness and trust. It means being willing to look for Him in the mundane and the miraculous, in the ordinary and the extraordinary. It means believing that He is present in every moment, even when He feels distant. It means trusting that He is working all things together for good, even when we cannot see it.

King David captured this idea in Psalm 139: "Where can I go from your Spirit? Where can I flee from your presence? If I go up to the heavens, you are there; if I make my bed in the depths, you are there." David understood that God is present in every season, in every circumstance, in

every high and every low. He recognized that no matter where life takes us—whether we are soaring on the mountaintop or trudging through the valley—God's presence is constant. He is always with us, working in every season for our good. This realization is both comforting and challenging. It comforts us by reminding us that we are never alone, but it also challenges us to trust in God's plan, even when that plan takes us through difficult or uncertain times.

Life's seasons are not random. Each one serves a purpose in God's overarching plan for our lives. Seasons of joy remind us of His blessings and encourage us to cultivate gratitude. Seasons of sorrow, though painful, can deepen our faith and reliance on Him. Seasons of growth are often the times when we draw closest to God, learning more about who He is and who He has called us to be. And seasons of waiting, though frustrating, teach us patience, perseverance, and trust in God's perfect timing.

In every season, God is teaching us something. He uses the highs and the lows, the successes and the failures, to reveal more of Himself to us. Sometimes, we may not understand what He is doing, but trusting that nothing is wasted allows us to embrace each season as a vital part of our spiritual journey. Whether we are in a time of abundance or scarcity, peace or struggle, God is using that season to mold us into the image of Christ.

It's easy to see God's hand in the good times, when everything is going smoothly and blessings seem to flow. But in the difficult seasons, it can be harder to recognize His presence. We may wonder why we are going through trials or feel abandoned in our suffering. Yet, it is often in these hard times that God does His most transformative work. In seasons of pain or confusion, God refines us, stripping away the things that distract us from Him and drawing us closer to His heart.

The apostle Paul speaks to this process of refinement in Romans 5:3-4, where he writes, "We also glory in tribulations, knowing that tribulation produces perseverance; and perseverance, character; and character, hope." Our struggles are not meaningless. They produce in us qualities that can only be developed through hardship—perseverance, character, and hope. God uses every trial to shape us into people of deeper faith, people who reflect His character more fully.

Seasons of waiting, too, are rich with purpose. Though waiting can be one of the hardest things to endure, it is also one of the most powerful ways God works in our lives. In the waiting, God teaches us to trust His timing rather than our own. He shows us that He is in control, even when we feel like life is at a standstill. Waiting stretches our faith, as we learn to rely on God's promises rather than our own understanding of the situation.

During these seasons of waiting, it's important to remember that God's silence is not absence. Just because we do not see immediate results does not mean God is not at work. Often, God is doing His most important work behind the scenes, preparing us for the next season or opening doors that we do not yet see. Trusting that nothing is wasted allows us to rest in the assurance that God is working, even when we can't perceive it.

In every season, God is inviting us to draw closer to Him. The challenges we face are not meant to push us away from God, but to pull us into a deeper relationship with Him. When we trust that nothing is wasted, we begin to see every season as an opportunity to grow in our faith, to deepen our trust, and to experience God's grace in new ways.

Recognizing God's presence in every season also shifts our perspective. Instead of viewing life's ups and downs as arbitrary, we begin to see them as part of a larger story that God is writing. We can approach each season with a sense of purpose, knowing that God is using it to accomplish His will in our lives. This perspective frees us from the fear of the unknown and the frustration of unmet expectations, as we rest in the knowledge that God's plans for us are always good, even when they are not what we expected.

Finally, trusting that nothing is wasted helps us live with a sense of hope. No matter what season we find ourselves in—whether it's one of joy, sorrow, growth, or waiting—we can have confidence that God is at work. We can face each day with the assurance that He is weaving every experience into a greater tapestry of His grace and glory. And as we trust Him in every season, we are drawn deeper into the fullness of the life He has for us.

7
Moving Forward with Faith

LIFE OFTEN CONFRONTS us with moments that challenge our deepest beliefs. We envision paths for ourselves, make plans, set goals, and pray for guidance, only to find that things do not unfold as expected. It is in these moments, when life seems to take a turn away from our desires, that we encounter divine disappointment. Our faith is tested not just by the existence of these disappointments, but by how we choose to respond to them.

Faith is more than a mental exercise; it is a posture of the heart, a decision to trust God even when the way forward is obscured by shadows. Faith is the willingness to say, "I don't understand, but I trust." It is a decision to move forward, step by step, holding onto the promises of a God who never changes, even when everything around us is shifting.

Moving forward with faith requires more than just a passive acceptance of our circumstances. It involves actively seeking God in the midst of our pain, bringing our broken dreams and unmet expectations to Him, and asking for His perspective. It is about trusting that He is at work, even when the evidence is not immediately apparent, and believing that He is leading us toward something far greater than what we had imagined.

This journey is not about denying the reality of our pain or pretending that everything is okay. It is about being honest with God about where we are and allowing Him to meet us in that place. It is about recognizing that while we may not understand the path, we can trust the One who leads us on it. It is about embracing the truth that our disappointments are not dead ends but divinely orchestrated redirections.

Faith also involves a willingness to relinquish control, to let go of our need to have all the answers, and to surrender to the sovereignty of a loving Father who knows what is best. It is an act of courage to trust that God is weaving every thread of our lives into a beautiful tapestry, even when all we can see are the tangled knots.

The Bible is filled with stories of men and women who moved forward in faith despite great uncertainty. Abraham left his home for a land he did not know, trusting in God's promise. Moses led the Israelites out of Egypt, facing an unknown future in the wilderness. Ruth walked into a foreign land with Naomi, believing that God would provide. Each step of faith was a step into the unknown, but it was also a step toward God's greater purpose.

These stories remind us that moving forward with faith is not a one-time decision but a daily choice. It is waking up each morning and choosing to trust God with our lives, our futures, and our hearts. It is believing that He is with us, that He is for us, and that He is working all things together for our good.

Faith does not require that we have it all figured out. It requires that we trust the One who does. It calls us to take the next step, even when we cannot see the full path, to believe that God is guiding us, even when the way seems unclear. It invites us to live with open hands, ready to receive whatever God has for us, knowing that His plans are always better than our own.

As we learn to move forward with faith, we discover that God is with us in every step, in every moment, in every breath. We find that His grace is sufficient for our every need, that His strength is made perfect in our weakness, and that His love never fails. We begin to see our disappointments not as setbacks, but as setups for His glory and our growth.

Reframing Disappointment as Divine Direction

Disappointments can feel like roadblocks, stopping us in our tracks, leaving us questioning what went wrong. Yet, what if these very moments are God's way of guiding us toward a path that we would not have chosen but that is ultimately for our best? What if our unmet expectations are actually divine appointments, opportunities for growth, and invitations to a deeper walk with God?

To reframe disappointment as divine direction, we must first recognize that God is always at work in our lives, even when we cannot see it. He is constantly orchestrating events, relationships, and circumstances to fulfill His purposes for us. This does not mean that God causes our pain, but it does mean that He is never caught off guard by it. He is always moving, always working, always guiding us toward a future filled with His hope and promise.

The story of Ruth offers a compelling illustration of this truth. After the loss of her husband, Ruth could have easily given in to despair. Her life, as she knew it, was over. Yet, she chose to follow her mother-in-law, Naomi, back to Bethlehem, a place she did not know and among people she had never met. What seemed like a desperate move was, in fact, a step toward God's provision and blessing. Ruth's willingness to follow God, even in her grief, led her to Boaz, her kinsman-redeemer, and positioned her in the lineage of Jesus Christ.

God often uses our disappointments to redirect us toward something far greater than we could imagine. The closed door is not a sign of rejection but a redirection to a better path. Joseph's life is another powerful example. Betrayed by his brothers, sold into slavery, and imprisoned under false accusations, his life seemed like a series of tragic events. Yet, God was at work, using each of these setbacks to position Joseph to save his family and many others during a time of famine. What his brothers intended for evil, God used for good (Genesis 50:20).

This perspective allows us to see our disappointments not as failures but as faith-building opportunities. They are moments that invite us to trust God more deeply, to seek His face more earnestly, and to rely on His strength more fully. When we begin to see our disappointments as divine directions, we start to recognize that God is always leading us, even when the way seems unclear.

Reframing disappointment as divine direction also invites us to let go of our need to understand everything. We do not have to know why things happened the way they did; we simply need to trust that God is in control. We may never fully understand the reasons behind our disappointments, but we can be confident that God is working all things together for our good.

This shift in perspective does not come easily. It requires a deliberate choice to see beyond the immediate pain and to look for God's hand at work. It requires us to trust that He is weaving all things together for a purpose far greater than we can comprehend. It means believing that God's plans for us are better than our own and that He is guiding us every step of the way.

When we reframe our disappointments as divine directions, we also begin to experience a new level of peace and freedom. We find ourselves less attached to our own plans and more open to what God is doing. We discover that His ways are higher than our ways, and His thoughts are higher than our thoughts (Isaiah 55:9). We learn to embrace the unexpected, knowing that God is always leading us, even in the detours.

This perspective invites us to release our grip on our desires, to trust in God's sovereignty, and to move forward with faith, believing that He is guiding us toward a future filled with hope. It calls us to look beyond the disappointments of today and to focus on the promises of tomorrow. It is a call to walk by faith, not by sight, trusting that God's plans for us are always good, even when the path is unclear.

Accepting What God Allows

Accepting what God allows is one of the most profound and challenging aspects of faith. It is easy to trust God when life is going well, but what about when our dreams are shattered, our prayers seem unanswered, and our hearts are broken? What does it mean to accept what God allows, and how do we do it?

Acceptance does not mean that we have to like or agree with everything that happens in our lives. It does not mean that we become passive or resigned to our circumstances. Instead, it means choosing to trust God, even when we do not understand His ways. It means believing that He is good, even when life is hard, and that He is with us, even when we feel alone.

To accept what God allows is to surrender our need for control and to rest in His sovereignty. It is to say, "God, I trust You, even when I do not understand. I believe You are at work, even when I cannot see it. I know You are good, even when my circumstances are not." It is a posture of humility and trust, a willingness to let go of our plans and to embrace His will.

Job's story offers a powerful example of what it means to accept what God allows. After losing everything—his wealth, his children, his health—Job chose to worship God, saying, "The Lord gave, and the Lord has taken away; blessed be the name of the Lord" (Job 1:21). Job did not understand why he was suffering, but he chose to trust God's character. He believed that God was still worthy of praise, even in the midst of his pain.

This kind of acceptance is not easy. It requires a daily decision to trust God, even when we do not understand His ways. It means bringing our questions, our fears, and our pain to Him, and allowing His presence to fill the gaps of our understanding. It means choosing to believe that He is with us, that He is for us, and that He is working all things together for our good.

Accepting what God allows also means being open to the unexpected. It means being willing to let go of our preconceived notions of how our lives should unfold and being willing to embrace the journey that God has for us. It means being ready to see HIs hand at work in the most unlikely places and to trust that He is guiding us, even when the path is uncertain.

When we accept what God allows, we find freedom. We find the freedom to let go of our need to control every outcome, the freedom to trust in His goodness, and the freedom to rest in His love. We find that His grace is sufficient, His strength is perfect, and His presence is enough.

Acceptance does not mean that we will never feel pain, disappointment, or sorrow. It means we bring those feelings to God, trusting that He understands, that He cares, and that He is with us. It means we hold onto His promises, even when life does not make sense, and we choose to believe that He is faithful, even when our faith feels weak.

As we learn to accept what God allows, we discover that He is with us in every moment, in every season, and in every circumstance. We find that His love never fails, His grace is always sufficient, and His promises are always true. And we learn to trust Him more deeply, to love Him more fully, and to follow Him more closely, even when the way is hard.

8
Worshipping Through the 'No'

IT'S OFTEN IN the quietest moments of our deepest frustrations that we hear the most transformative words: "no." You've asked, pleaded, cried out for a "yes," and yet, there you stand with nothing but the resounding echo of silence or a door gently closed in your face. How do we, as Christians, navigate these moments when God's answer isn't what we had hoped? How do we find true worship in the midst of disappointment? This chapter invites you to explore a dynamic form of worship—a devotion that flourishes not in the abundance of "yes" but in the fertile ground of faith that grows from "no."

When we think of worship, our minds might jump to the music of Sunday morning or the whispered prayers of gratitude. However, worship is so much more than songs sung or words spoken. It's a state of the heart, a posture of surrender that says, "God, I trust You, even when I don't understand You." Worship through a "no" demands a reorientation of our expectations. It's the journey of redefining success not by outcomes but by our unyielding pursuit of closeness with God.

Consider for a moment the saints of old, who lived exuberant lives of faith punctuated by divine "nos." Abraham was promised descendants as numerous as the stars but asked to sacrifice his only son. Mary, the mother of Jesus, gave an unconditional "yes" to God, only to watch her beloved son endure a brutal crucifixion. Their unwavering dedication amid such profound "nos" becomes a testimony for us, inspiring a worshipful heart that recognizes God's sovereignty beyond our understanding.

In our modern lives, God's "no" often feels like a contradiction to our faith. We might wrestle with doubt, questioning, "Did I do something wrong?" or "Is my faith not enough?" But what if we reframed these doubts into acts of worship? This doesn't mean blindly accepting every difficult situation as something we should glorify, but rather, embracing the mystery of divine wisdom that invites us to a deeper relationship. Let go of what might have been and find truth in what is, knowing that God is with us even when He seems silent.

To worship through the "no," we must cultivate an intimate reliance on God—a shift from trusting Him for the things we want to trusting Him for who He is. This is mirrored beautifully in the life of Job, who faced unimaginable loss and yet proclaimed, "Though He slay me, yet will I hope in Him." Job's story is not an invitation to masochism but a call to align our hearts with God's purposes rather than our plans. There is a sacredness in yielding to God's "no," a worship that affirms His ultimate goodness and faithful presence.

Sometimes, worship through the "no" requires a fresh perspective, the lens by which we view our circumstances. We are invited to see beyond the immediate sting of a closed door to perceive the broader picture of God's craftsmanship in our lives. It's acknowledging that our understanding is limited and accepting that His plans, though hidden from us now, work towards a far greater glory. As Isaiah 55:8-9 reminds us, God's thoughts are not our thoughts, nor His ways our ways. Worship, therefore, is the humble acceptance of this truth, letting it guide our responses to every "no" we encounter.

It's okay to bring our disappointment, our confusion, and our heartache directly to God. Honest prayer is a profound act of worship—not because our lament changes God's mind, but because it changes our hearts. In the rawness of transparency, we meet

God in our vulnerability, offering Him the pieces of our shattered expectations. Through this act, worship becomes a bridge, connecting the gap between our perceived lack and God's rich sufficiency.

One practical way to engage in this form of worship is by cultivating gratitude, even when it feels most counterintuitive. Start small, thanking God for the simple gifts that often go unnoticed amidst the pursuit of what we lack. Gratitude shifts our focus, helping us to affirm God's goodness, which transcends the immediate and spans the eternal. It writes a narrative of hope, even in the darkest chapters of our lives.

There is also power in community. Sharing our stories with others, listening to their journeys, and witnessing their unwavering faith can reignite our own. As you gather with fellow believers, let worship arise collectively, whether through prayer, song, or simple fellowship. Through community, we are reminded that we are not alone, and together, we hold on to the promise that God is weaving a tapestry of redemption through each "no."

As you embark on this journey of worshipping through the "no," may you find a new dimension of faith that shines brighter because of the struggles you've faced. May God's peace envelope you, even when answers elude and skies remain gray. Remember, the essence of worship is not in securing what you desire but in entrusting every part of your being to a loving Creator who holds the universe—and your heart—in His capable hands.

In the end, it is the consistent hum of faith, quietly affirming, "I trust You," that becomes our song of worship. It echoes through the silences and the uncertainties, aligning our hearts with God's eternal rhythm. Indeed, worshipping through the "no" might just turn out to be the grandest symphony of faith any heart can sing.

The Power of Praise in Hard Times

The Power of Praise in Hard Times is far more than just a spiritual catchphrase—it's a lifeline when the storms of life rage and the weight of a divine "No" feels like too much to bear. In those moments when it seems like your efforts are futile and your prayers have collided with an immovable wall, praise becomes more than a response—it becomes your strategy. It's not about accepting defeat but finding strength by lifting God's name, even when your heart is heavy with unmet expectations.

Praise in challenging seasons stems from recognizing that God's wisdom far exceeds our own understanding. When faced with a reality that doesn't align with your prayers, a powerful shift occurs when you turn your attention away from what you didn't receive and focus on what God has already done. This shift isn't about denial or forced positivity; it's about trusting in the sovereignty of God, knowing that His plans are always working for your good, even when you can't see it. Through praise, you proclaim that God is still faithful, no matter what the circumstances may look like.

Personally, I've learned this truth on a deep level. After losing my legs and finding myself in a new reality where I had to depend on others in ways I never anticipated, I never stopped praising God. In the face of emotional and physical challenges, praise became my anchor. It helped heal my heart and renew my mind, offering strength where I felt weak. Every moment of worship became a place where I could release my frustration and confusion, and in turn, receive God's peace and comfort. I realized that praising Him didn't change my situation, but it transformed how I navigated it.

Praise has been my path to healing, not just physically but emotionally and spiritually. It became a way to rise above my circumstances, shifting my perspective from what I had lost to the grace and strength I had gained. Worship has renewed me, restoring hope and allowing me to trust God's purpose for my life, even when the road looked different from what I had imagined.

Praising God in hard times is not about pretending everything is okay; it's about acknowledging the pain while still lifting up His name. It's about declaring that even in the midst of suffering, God's presence is with you. When you praise through hardship, it's a direct statement of faith—a bold proclamation that your hope isn't anchored in outcomes, but in God's character. It creates space for healing, inviting God to minister to your wounds in ways nothing else can.

When you choose to praise in the face of adversity, it stops the downward spiral of despair. It shifts the atmosphere of your heart from one of hopelessness to one of trust. Scripture reminds us that God inhabits the praises of His people, and there is power in that truth. When we lift our voices, even in pain, we open ourselves to His presence in a way that strengthens us beyond our understanding.

Worship doesn't guarantee that your circumstances will immediately change, but it changes how you approach them. It offers a renewed strength to endure the hardship, allowing you to stand firm even when the answer is "No." Praise anchors you to the truth that God is good, even when life doesn't feel that way. It reminds you that His love and grace are sufficient, and that His presence is more powerful than the trials you face.

In the Psalms, we see this dynamic play out repeatedly. Time and again, David would bring his fears, doubts, and complaints to God, but he always circled back to praise. He didn't deny his pain, but he chose to worship through it, knowing that God's presence was his true refuge. In the same way, praise becomes your refuge, your place of strength when life feels overwhelming.

Praise also reminds you that God is at work, even when the outcome doesn't align with your desires. It keeps your heart soft, preventing bitterness from taking root. It's in these moments of worship that you find the grace to accept the "No" and trust that God's plan is greater than you can imagine. Praise becomes your declaration that, despite the unanswered prayers, God's hand is still guiding your life.

In the end, worship is not just about what you receive, but about who you become. It strengthens your character, refines your faith, and deepens your relationship with God. Praise doesn't remove the pain, but it positions you to see God's hand in the midst of it. It transforms your heart, filling it with hope and trust in the One who never fails.

Through praise, I've experienced renewal and healing, not because my situation drastically changed, but because God met me where I was. His presence became my source of strength, and His faithfulness, my song. Praise in hard times is not just a response—it's a powerful act of trust in the God who sees, knows, and loves you through every "No."

Strengthening Your Heart Through Worship

Strengthening your heart through worship is an invitation to realign your perspective, especially when confronted with God's "no." As believers, we often face moments when our prayers seem to remain unanswered, leaving us in a whirlwind of disappointment, doubt, and frustration. Yet, worship in the midst of these challenging seasons holds a transformative power—one that doesn't just help us cope but enables us to rise above unmet expectations. Through worship, we shift our focus from what we lack to who God is, from temporary circumstances to His eternal faithfulness.

Worship, especially during adversity, is an act of defiance against despair. When we choose to praise God despite our circumstances, we are declaring that our faith is not dependent on favorable outcomes but anchored in His unchanging nature. This type of worship doesn't deny our pain or hide our struggles; rather, it creates space for both lament and reverence, pain and praise. As we worship, we allow God's presence to meet us in our weakness, strengthening our hearts with His love and assurance.

Consider the story of King David after the loss of his child with Bathsheba. In a moment of deep grief and personal failure, David sought God in fasting and prayer, pleading for his child's life. But when the answer was 'no' and his child passed away, David's response was not to retreat into bitterness or despair. Instead, he went into the house of the Lord and worshiped (2 Samuel 12:20). This act of worship wasn't a denial of his pain but a profound demonstration of trust in God's sovereignty. David's heart was strengthened not by an answered prayer, but by his unwavering belief that God was still good, even in the midst of his deepest sorrow.

Worship, then, becomes more than just a ritual; it's a choice to align ourselves with God's greater plan. It's a declaration that we trust His wisdom, even when His answer is not what we had hoped for. Through worship, we are reminded that His "no" is not a rejection but an alignment with a purpose beyond what we can immediately see. This shift in perspective allows us to embrace the process of faith, learning that God's grace is often most evident when our prayers seem unanswered.

Gratitude plays a vital role in this transformation. Even when life feels incomplete or disappointing, choosing to thank God for His faithfulness reorients our hearts. Gratitude invites us to see beyond our current pain and acknowledge the blessings that surround us. It opens the door to a deeper level of worship, one that is rooted in trust and sustained by the knowledge that God has always provided and will continue to do so. By practicing gratitude, we fortify our hearts, making worship not just a response to joy but a foundation for enduring hardship.

Worship also reminds us of who we are in Christ. In moments of rejection or disappointment, we may be tempted to question our worth or standing before God. But worship calls us back to our identity as His beloved children. Our value is not defined by our circumstances or what we receive; it's grounded in the unchanging reality that we are loved by God. This truth strengthens our hearts, giving us the confidence to face even the most difficult "no" with the assurance that we are secure in Him.

In addition to personal worship, the power of collective worship cannot be overlooked. While we find strength individually, there's something uniquely powerful about joining with others in praise. The shared experience of worship within a community serves as a reminder that we are not walking this path alone. When we lift our voices together, we are encouraged by the faith of those around us, and their praise strengthens our own. Their songs of hope and trust echo into our hearts, reminding us that even in our darkest moments, we are surrounded by a cloud of witnesses who have walked this road before us and found God to be faithful.

Through worship, we also gain a deeper understanding of God's sovereignty. It is in these moments of surrender—when we lift our hands in praise despite not understanding His plans—that we find peace. Worship teaches us to trust in the mystery of God's will, knowing that He sees the full picture when we can only see a fragment. This trust doesn't come easily, but as we worship, we learn to release our need for control and rest in the assurance that God is working all things together for our good, even when the path is unclear.

Worship fuels hope. It strengthens our hearts by keeping our eyes fixed on the promise of God's faithfulness. Even in seasons of waiting or unanswered prayers, worship reminds us that God is still at work. It builds anticipation, teaching us to trust in the "not yet" while holding onto the belief that God's best is yet to come. Every time we choose to worship, we are declaring that we believe in His goodness, even when we cannot see the full picture.

In essence, worship is both a practice and a posture. It's an intentional choice to turn our eyes from our circumstances and place them on the One who holds our future. Through worship, we find strength to face each "no" with courage, trusting that God's plan for our lives is far greater than anything we could imagine. Worship doesn't necessarily change our circumstances, but it changes us—strengthening our hearts, anchoring our hope, and drawing us closer to the heart of God.

Conclusion

As we reach the end of this journey, we are reminded that walking with God is both a mystery and a marvel. It is a path marked by moments of breathtaking beauty and heartbreaking pain, by seasons of clarity and seasons of confusion, by days of rejoicing and nights of weeping. Yet through it all, we are invited to trust in a God who is faithful, who is good, and who is always with us.

We have explored the reality of divine disappointment, the mystery of miracles, the sovereignty of God, and the challenge of reconciling faith with reality. We have considered the lessons from Paul's thorn, the assurance that all things work together for good, and the call to move forward with faith. Each chapter has invited us to trust God more deeply, to see our struggles through His eyes, and to believe that He is always at work, even when we cannot see it.

This journey is not about finding all the answers but about knowing the One who holds them. It is not about avoiding pain but about finding God's presence in the midst of it. It is not about getting everything we want, but about discovering that God Himself is everything we need.

As we move forward, may we find the courage to trust God with our unanswered questions, to embrace His grace in our moments of weakness, and to rest in His love in every season of life. May we learn to see our disappointments as divine directions, to accept what God allows with a heart full of trust, and to walk by faith, not by sight, believing that His plans for us are always good.

May we remember that God is always writing a story far greater than we could ever imagine. A story that includes both the highs and the lows, the miracles, and the waiting. A story that is ultimately about His glory and our growth, His purpose, and our joy.

May we hold onto the truth that God is with us in every moment, in every step, and in every breath. He is with us in the waiting, in the wondering, and in the walking. He is with us in the joy and the sorrow, in the certainty and the doubt, in the victories, and in the valleys.

As we continue this journey, may we find strength in His presence, hope in His promises, and peace in His sovereignty. May we discover, in every moment, that He is always enough. And may we rest in the assurance that He is working all things together for our good and His glory, both now and forevermore.

Appendix A: Appendix

In moments when our hearts ache with unmet expectations, the journey to finding peace can feel like an uphill battle. This appendix offers a collection of reflections and insights aimed at helping believers navigate these challenging times. While previous chapters have delved into specific aspects of dealing with divine disappointment, this section serves as a concise companion for ongoing reflection and encouragement.

Let's explore the importance of trusting in God's unwavering presence and love, even when clarity seems elusive. Remember, it's natural to question and seek understanding when life doesn't unfold as planned, especially through the lens of faith.

1. Trusting Beyond Understanding

In your walk of faith, it's essential to recognize that God's plans often transcend our immediate understanding. While this truth might initially seem daunting, embracing it can liberate us from the endless cycle of questioning "Why?" and move us towards a peaceful acceptance of "What next?"

2. Leaning Into Divine Grace

When faced with personal thorns, like Paul, we're invited not only to endure but to grow. The journey isn't about striving for perfection but acknowledging our weaknesses and allowing God's strength to shine through them. This understanding transforms our imperfections into avenues for divine grace.

3. Embracing the Journey

The path of faith is not a direct line from point A to B. Each twist, turn, and unexpected halt holds potential lessons that can draw us closer to the divine. Embrace the journey with an openness to learn, and see how these experiences can refine and strengthen your faith.

4. Empowered by Community

Don't underestimate the power of walking this journey with others. Connection with fellow believers provides encouragement, different perspectives, and a reminder that you're not alone in your struggles or your hopes.

5. Celebrating Little Miracles

While grand miracles may sporadically dot our lives, the everyday miracles found in simple, ordinary moments can sometimes hold the most profound significance. Celebrate these small victories as gentle reminders of God's intricate involvement in the tapestry of our lives.

In conclusion, while divine disappointments may not have easy resolutions, they invite us to deepen our trust, expand our faith, and open our hearts to God's enduring promise. May this appendix offer comfort and courage as you step forward, nourished by the reminder that you are held by a love beyond measure.

Appendix B: 30 Days of Faith Confessions and Encouragement

Day 1:

- *Confession*: I am provided for by my Heavenly Father, and all my needs are met according to His riches in glory.
- *Encouragement*: God's provision is abundant and faithful. Even when it seems like there's not enough, trust that He is working on your behalf.

Day 2:

- *Confession*: I walk in perfect peace, and fear has no place in my life.
- *Encouragement*: When fear tries to creep in, declare God's peace over your mind and heart. His peace is greater than any fear.

Day 3:

- *Confession*: By His stripes, I am healed. I stand on God's promise of healing.
- *Encouragement*: Whether you're dealing with physical pain or emotional wounds, God is your healer. Keep trusting in His power to restore.

Day 4:

- *Confession*: The joy of the Lord is my strength. I will not be discouraged, for He renews my energy.
- *Encouragement*: When you feel weary, tap into the joy that comes from knowing God. His joy gives you supernatural strength.

Day 5:

- *Confession*: God is guiding me. I trust Him completely to lead me on the right path.
- *Encouragement*: Even when life is uncertain, God is in control. Trust that He knows exactly where you need to go.

Day 6:

- *Confession*: I am covered by God's protection. No harm will come near me.
- *Encouragement*: God's protection is your shield. In moments of danger, rest in the safety of His wings.

Day 7:

- *Confession*: I am more than a conqueror through Christ. I have victory in every area of my life.
- *Encouragement*: No matter what challenge you face, victory is already yours. Walk in the authority Christ has given you.

Day 8:

- *Confession*: I have eternal life through Christ, and my hope is secure in Him.
- *Encouragement*: The promise of eternal life gives you hope that goes beyond the trials of this world. Your future is secure.

Day 9:

- *Confession*: I am never alone. God is with me wherever I go.
- *Encouragement*: God's presence is always with you, even in the most difficult times. You are never abandoned.

Day 10:

- *Confession*: I live by faith and not by sight. I trust in God's promises even when I cannot see the outcome.
- *Encouragement*: Keep your focus on God's promises, not your circumstances. Faith sees beyond the temporary.

Day 11:

- *Confession*: I am strong in the Lord and in the power of His might. No weapon formed against me will prosper.
- *Encouragement*: God's strength is available to you every day. No opposition can stand when you are covered by His power.

Day 12:

- *Confession*: I am blessed in every area of my life. God's favor surrounds me like a shield.
- *Encouragement*: God's favor isn't limited to specific moments; it's with you daily. Trust that His blessings are at work even when you don't see them yet.

Day 13:

- *Confession*: I have the mind of Christ, and my thoughts are aligned with His will.
- *Encouragement*: In moments of confusion, ask for the mind of Christ. He gives clarity and direction, replacing uncertainty with purpose.

Day 14:

- *Confession*: My faith is growing stronger each day. I will not waver in believing God's promises for my life.
- *Encouragement*: Like a muscle, your faith grows when you exercise it. Stay steadfast, knowing that God is faithful to fulfill His promises.

Day 15:

- *Confession*: God's grace is sufficient for me. His power is made perfect in my weakness.
- *Encouragement*: When you feel weak, rely on God's grace. His strength shines through when we surrender our limitations to Him.

Day 16:

- *Confession*: God is my provider, and I lack nothing. He supplies all my needs according to His riches.
- *Encouragement*: Even when you face lack, remember that God is your source. He has abundant resources to provide everything you need.

Day 17:

- *Confession*: My heart is filled with God's peace, which guards my mind and soul in Christ Jesus.
- *Encouragement*: Anxiety has no power over you. The peace of God will guard your heart and mind as you trust in Him.

Day 18:

- *Confession*: I am filled with God's joy. This joy is my strength and gives me the energy to pursue His purposes.
- *Encouragement*: Joy is more than an emotion; it's a divine source of strength. Lean on God's joy to energize your spirit, even in difficult seasons.

Day 19:

- *Confession*: I am God's workmanship, created in Christ Jesus for good works. My life has purpose and meaning.
- *Encouragement*: You were created for a reason. God has a unique purpose for your life, and every step you take is part of His plan.

Day 20:

- *Confession*: The Lord is my shepherd, and I shall not want. He leads me beside still waters and restores my soul.
- *Encouragement*: Let God lead you to rest and restoration. His care for you is personal, and He will restore your soul when you feel depleted.

Day 21:

- *Confession*: I walk by faith and not by sight. God's promises are more real to me than my circumstances.
- *Encouragement*: Faith transcends what you can see. Even when circumstances seem overwhelming, trust in God's promises, which never fail.

Day 22:

- *Confession*: I am a child of God, deeply loved and chosen by Him. Nothing can separate me from His love.
- *Encouragement*: No mistake, hardship, or challenge can distance you from God's love. You are His beloved, and His love for you is eternal.

Day 23:

- *Confession*: I am courageous and bold. God has not given me a spirit of fear, but of power, love, and a sound mind.
- *Encouragement*: Fear has no place in your life. God has given you boldness and the power to move forward with confidence.

Day 24:

- *Confession*: I am planted by streams of living water, and I bear fruit in every season. My life prospers under God's care.
- *Encouragement*: Even in challenging times, God causes you to flourish. Stay connected to Him, and you will see growth and fruitfulness.

Day 25:

- *Confession*: My hope is in the Lord, and I will not be disappointed. I trust Him with my future.
- *Encouragement*: Hope is never wasted when it is placed in God. His plans for your future are good, and He will never let you down.

Day 26:

- *Confession*: I live in the overflow of God's goodness. His blessings are chasing me down and overtaking me.
- *Encouragement*: God's blessings aren't limited—they overflow in abundance. Trust that He is showering His goodness over your life.

Day 27:

- *Confession*: God's promises are yes and amen in Christ Jesus. I stand on His Word, knowing that every promise will come to pass.
- *Encouragement*: God never fails to fulfill His promises. His Word is true, and you can trust that everything He has spoken will be accomplished.

Day 28:

- *Confession*: I have divine wisdom and understanding. God is giving me insight and direction for every decision I need to make.
- *Encouragement*: In times of uncertainty, trust that God is giving you wisdom. He will guide your steps and provide clarity.

Day 29:

- *Confession*: I am a new creation in Christ. Old things have passed away, and all things have become new.
- *Encouragement*: No matter your past, you are a new creation. Embrace the fresh start God has given you and walk in your new identity.

Day 30:

- *Confession*: I am victorious in Christ. Every battle I face has already been won through Him.
- *Encouragement*: The victory is yours because of Christ. Walk confidently, knowing that you are fighting from a place of victory, not for it.

Using These Confessions

1. **Declare Daily**: Set aside time each morning to declare the confession for the day. Speak it out loud with confidence.
2. **Reflect**: Take a few moments to reflect on the confession and how it applies to your current situation. Write down any thoughts, prayers, or insights.
3. **Pray**: Use the confession as a starting point for your prayer. Ask God to strengthen your faith in that area and thank Him for His promises.
4. **Meditate on the Promise**: Throughout the day, meditate on God's promises that correspond with the confession. Keep His Word in your heart and mind.
5. **Stay Consistent**: Consistency is key. As you go through these 30 days, you will see your faith grow, your mindset shift, and God's promises manifest in your life.

By dedicating 30 days to these faith-building confessions and encouragements, you will reinforce your trust in God's Word, experience His promises firsthand, and walk with renewed confidence in His plan for your life.

Notes

Made in the USA
Columbia, SC
30 October 2024

45245347R10057